The Catholic Church Story: Changing and Changeless

Father Edward Day, C.SS.R.

Liguori Publications
One Liguori Drive
Liguori, Mo. 63057

Imprimi Potest:
Edmund T. Langton, C.SS.R.
Provincial, St. Louis Province
Redemptorist Fathers
September 2, 1975

Imprimatur:
St. Louis, September 5, 1975
+ Charles R. Koester
Auxiliary Bishop of St. Louis

Library of Congress Catalog Card Number: 75-27612

4th Printing, July, 1977

Printed in U.S.A.

Cover photo by Kathleen M. Graham

Dedication

To my Redemptorist brothers, whose brains I have picked and whose patience I have brittled, and to my loyal relatives and friends:

All know that without their love and confidence this book would never have been written.

Table of Contents

Foreword

"Lots of changes, no improvements," so a venerable Redemptorist lay Brother of happy memory was heard to mutter when he learned of the appointments of several new pastors in the St. Louis Province of the Congregation of the Most Holy Redeemer. One might amusedly sympathize with his canny cynicism, but Brother's logic left something to be desired.

"Change" and "improvement" are not synonomous terms. Yet change is part and parcel of the human situation.

When God "emptied himself" and came to the world as the man, Jesus Christ, he exposed himself to all the liabilities of being a Jew in the 1st century. He shackled himself with the geography, the naïveté, the aspirations, and the bigotries of the kingdom of Judea. And that was hampering indeed, because he brought Good News for all men of all times. In trying to make a handful of Palestinian Jews believe that the Father had sent his Son to die and rise from the dead for the sins of mankind, Christ brought about the very sacrificial act that saved mankind. Because of their geography, their naïveté, their aspirations, and their bigotries, this handful of men in this Jewish corner of the world crucified him. His death was a failure to communicate, but a happy failure because it paid the price of all men's sins. Salvation came from the Jews.

During his brief life, Jesus Christ, lodged in history by a humble birth and a bloody death, commissioned followers to carry on his efforts to communicate his Good News not merely to the Jews but to all men for all times. These followers composed his fragile fellowship, the Church. They were fragile because they were human with their own geography, naïveté, aspirations, and bigotries. They were a fellowship because, despite their geography, naïveté, aspirations, and bigotries, they were united by a common confidence in Christ. To all men, throughout all ages, Christ commissioned them to communicate his Good News by proclamation, sacrament, and sacrifice. St. Paul, the self-styled superapostle, first saw the vast proportions

7

of Christ's commission. He first took the Good News to non-Jewish pagans. He won some; he lost some. He advised the fragile fellowship to be all things to all men to win all for Christ. But he knew that this formula was far from infallible. After all, he, a Tarsian tentmaker learned in Jewish lore, had tried to turn philosopher to bring sophisticated Athenians to Christ and he had failed. But failure could not fault his philosophy of being all to all.

Change can only bring improvement when it is tempered with the Spirit of the Good News. To temper it, change cannot be ignored; it must be confronted. This confrontation, with its successes and failures, is the chronicle of the fragile fellowship which we call the Catholic Church.

Since Jesus Christ rose to the Father, the Church has carried on his mission of proclaiming the Good News to all men throughout the ages. Its mission has been tempered by the limitations of human geography, naïveté, aspirations, and bigotries. Since his Ascension, the world has changed gradually but traumatically.

Beginning as a private cult, exposed to the insults of the majority, by the 5th century the fragile fellowship had overcome in the Western World. It became the official religion of the Roman Empire.

When that empire toppled in the West, the Church, as custodian of Greco-Roman culture, shaped barbarians into Christian gentlemen and preserved civilization throughout the Middle Ages. And that civilization of Charlemagne, Thomas Aquinas, Frederick II, and Dante was impressive indeed.

Closely allied, but sometimes in conflict, with the political powers that came to be, the Church became an attractive target for middle-class, medieval mavericks, urbanized merchant moneymakers, who were swiftly outgrowing their feudal milieu. In the 16th century they struck out at what they considered to be the Church's autocratic paternalism that seemed to shackle hankerings to be free. Throughout the 17th and 18th centuries these mavericks of feudalism cut down kings anointed by the Church.

Stripped of its monarchical protectors, the fragile fellowship found itself pummeled once again by a growing majority of disbelievers, new pagans who increasingly came to believe that this was the only world there was and, therefore, the Church's Good News was irrelevant.

In the second half of the 20th century the Catholic Church is faced with a pagan renaissance. The predominant philosophy is aptly expressed by a popular beer commercial, "You only go around once in this life . . . . You've got to grab all the gusto you can." This change of human outlook does not represent improvement. Recent history proves horrifyingly well that where humanity is glorified as godly, all manner of devilish acts can be justified in its name. To temper these neopagan, humanistic aspirations with the leaven of divine kindness remains the seemingly Quixotic quest of the fragile fellowship. At a time when human physical science is practically caressing the creative power of God, his Good News alone remains the hope of humanity.

Heading each chapter of the text is a random list of names of members of the fragile fellowship. Some are saints, some are scholars, some are mavericks; all have tried, in their fragility, to witness to a fellowship with Christ. Investigating what they stood for will add flesh and blood dimensions to the Church's pilgrimage charted in these pages.

Following each chapter is a list of questions suggested by the text to stimulate discussion where this book is used in a study group. The short bibliography indicates avenues of further research for the reader who wishes to broaden his horizons on the trek through Church history.

Edward Day, C.SS.R.
Liguori, Missouri
April 18, 1975

The Catholic Church Story:
Changing and Changeless

Chapter I
In the Beginning Was Christ
and Christ Was the Church

Some of Christ's Fragile Fellowship

Peter (d. 64-68) — the Rock.
Paul (d. 68) — the superapostle.
Cornelius — the pagan convert who led the gentiles in.
James — bishop of Jerusalem, Jewish-Christian blockbuster.

The salvation of mankind is totally dependent upon the historical fact of Jesus Christ. Jesus Christ, true God and true Man, was born around the year 4 B.C. He died for all men on a Cross outside Jerusalem in the spring of the year 33 A.D. In order to bring the gift of forgiveness to all men to the end of time, our Lord founded a Church — a mystical continuation of himself. Though Christ physically ascended into heaven, his Church carried the Christ-life of sanctifying grace to all people who approached her seeking salvation. In Baptism the Church united them to Christ in his death and his Resurrection. In the Eucharist they nourished the Christ-life within them by feeding on his flesh. The Church carried Christ's pardon to all in the sacrament of Penance, and it sanctified life and death with the sacraments of Matrimony, Holy Orders, and the Anointing of the Sick.

That our Lord founded a Church which was to be a fellowship of his followers is clear from even a cursory reading of the New Testament. He chose a group of men to follow him, his apostles. Simon was renamed Peter (Rock), because he was to be the foundation of Christ's Church. The apostles were commissioned to carry the Good News of Christ's coming to the ends of the earth. They would speak not in their own name but in Christ's. Our Lord promised to remain with this fellowship to the end of time.

First Preaching

Ten days after Christ rose into heaven, on Pentecost, the Twelve obeyed his command and began to preach publicly in Jerusalem. By the power of the Holy Spirit, though they spoke in Aramaic, all the foreign-born Jews celebrating the Pentecostal feast in Jerusalem were able to understand them. St. Peter preached that the Messiah, predicted of old, had come and that their leaders had crucified him. Now they must acknowledge him by doing penance and by being baptized. A large number of Jews came to Christ that day through the words of his chief apostles (Acts 2). The Church was on its way.

The converts to Christ did not feel cut off from their fellow Jews. They simply felt that they lived in the fulfillment of the Old Testament in the age of the Messiah. They looked forward to his early return when his reign might triumph over all. In the meantime, they faithfully went to the Temple to worship God, their "Lord and Christ."

The New Jews

Nevertheless, they *were* different. The crucified Messiah was bound to become a stumbling block to the Jews. The Twelve who had witnessed his Resurrection directed this new group, not the Law nor the Jewish leaders. Though Christ's followers frequented the Temple, they also met privately in their homes for "the breaking of bread," the sacrifice the Savior had left them. This rite was a pledge of his return, for this bread became himself. This Eucharist was the bond that would hold them together until he came, for, sharing in his Body, they themselves became that Body which is the Church (1 Cor 10:16-17).

Judaism might have learned to live with the followers of Christ had not Stephen, in preaching Jesus, minimized the importance of the Temple. He emphasized the worship of God in spirit and in truth, not merely in the Temple that Solomon had built in Jerusalem — "not in houses made by hands does the Most High dwell" (Acts 7:48). Stephen was stoned for a preaching that was inevitable, and a persecution broke out against the fellowship of Christ in Jerusalem (Acts 8:1).

New Jews Called Christians

God's hand was in the persecution, for it forced most of Christ's followers to leave Jerusalem and go out into the world. When the Romans destroyed the Temple in 70 A.D., Christian-

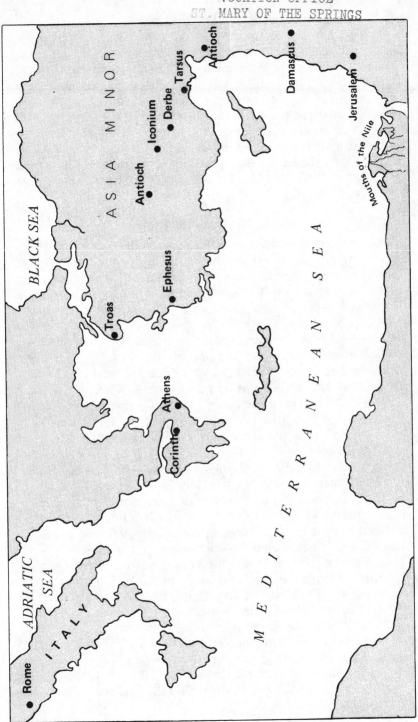

ity had spread well beyond the Holy City.

The fellowship of Christ fled north to Samaria and made many converts, for these Jews were not strongly attached to worship in far-off Jerusalem (Jn 4:20). They went to Antioch, in Syria, and there brought the Good News of Christ to pagans who were looking for salvation (Acts 11:19-20). Because they preached that the Lord Jesus was the Messiah, these northerners sensed the novelty of their teaching. They saw that they were more than mere Jews still awaiting the Messiah. The Messiah had come in Christ, so they proclaimed. Therefore, the people of Antioch called this Messianic group "Christians." The name stuck (Acts 11:26).

Paul, Apostle to the Pagans

A fire-eating Pharisee named Saul sensed the opposition there was to the Jewish faith in this Messianic community. Determining to crush it, he set out from Jerusalem for Damascus. En route, God miraculously converted him by striking him from his horse and crying, "Saul, Saul, why do you persecute me?" (Acts 9:1-9)

This Saul, the Pharisee, became the great St. Paul of Christianity. Paul had not had the opportunity to follow our Lord when he had been on earth, but he prided himself on the fact that Christ had called him to be an apostle. Though this man had held the cloaks of the executioners of Stephen, the deacon, Paul testified that the mercy of God had set him apart, even before his birth, as the one who would reveal Jesus Christ to the non-Jewish people, the gentiles (Gal 1:15-16).

To prepare himself for his mission to the gentiles, Paul retired to the Arabian desert where the Holy Spirit became his teacher, revealing to the apostle "unutterable utterances which no man is permitted to repeat" (2 Cor 12:1-4). His training completed, St. Paul returned to Damascus and forcefully preached the Lord Jesus Christ. In Jerusalem he worked among the Greek-speaking Jews, but the effectiveness of his message stirred up their hatred for this renegade Pharisee and they plotted to kill him. It was then that the Christians of Jerusalem decided to get Paul out of the city to the safety of his hometown of Tarsus in Asia Minor.

When Peter, after some reluctance, received the God-fearing Roman centurion, Cornelius, into the Church, the Holy Spirit showed the Messianic group that the salvation of Christ was for all men, not merely for the Jews (Acts 10:44-48). Missionary work is as old as the Church, for within the first few years of its

16

existence, the Holy Spirit sent Paul and Barnabas upon the foreign missions (Acts 13:2 ff.).

Paul Hits the Road for Christ

The first missionary journey of St. Paul took him from Antioch in Syria to the island of Cyprus. From Cyprus he sailed to the mainland of Asia Minor and traveled north to Antioch in Pisidia. Going from the Pisidian Antioch, through Iconium to Derbe, it was Paul's custom to bring the Good News of Christ first to the Jews, for salvation had come from the Jews. If his former coreligionists rejected his message, then he carried the Gospel of Christ to the gentiles, for Jesus had come to save all men. Though his converts were many, Paul once again succeeded in arousing the hatred of some of the Jews who regarded him as a fallen-away traitor. To silence his preaching, their efforts to raise a hue and cry against him were largely successful and the apostle, more than once, was forced to leave town (Acts 13:48-52).

On his second missionary journey, St. Paul traveled overland through Asia Minor and then sailed at Troas for the Macedonian shore in Europe. This trip took the apostle to Athens where he unsuccessfully tried to play the philosopher on the Areopagus. Noting that the Athenians worshiped "the unknown God" among their deities, he came, he said, to make this God, who had created the earth and all that was in it, known to them. However, the reception he received was far from enthusiastic, so he left Athens, leaving only a few converts behind (Acts 17:16-34).

Paul spent some 18 months at Corinth, working as a tentmaker during the week and preaching Jesus Christ on the Sabbath. Though he aroused the ire of many Jews, he also firmly established Christianity in that Achaean seaport. Paul then sailed from Corinth to Samos in Asia Minor and finally regained Antioch in Syria.

The apostle's third missionary voyage brought him to Ephesus. Here Paul became involved in new conflicts over Christ. Ephesus was internationally famous for its shrine to Diana, the goddess of the Ephesians. Paul, preaching monotheism, stirred up the silversmiths of the city against him, for these artisans made their living fashioning small souvenir idols of Diana for the pilgrims who came to her shrine. The hate of these pagans, together with the plotting of certain members of the Jewish community, forced Paul out of Ephesus (Acts 19).

From Ephesus, the apostle of the gentiles pressed on to Macedonia and once again journeyed through Greece.

When Paul finally returned to Jerusalem, only the troops of the Roman tribune saved him from being lynched by a Jewish mob that cornered him at the Temple (Acts 21:31). Paul was a Roman citizen, so he appealed to the emperor for a judgment of his innocence, a right attached to citizenship. Apparently, Paul was acquitted, for Pope Clement I (c. 92-101) tells us that the apostle left Rome and preached the Gospel as far west as Spain (*Epistle to the Corinthians*, 5:7). Finally, during the persecution of Nero, Paul gave his life for his faith in Rome (*Ibid.*, 6:1).

What Was the Good News?

What was the Good News that St. Paul preached? He carried the word that Jesus was the Christ, the Messiah. A man was saved by believing in Christ's death and Resurrection and by availing himself of it by being baptized. Paul underlined the real mystical union of the Christian with Christ because he had been baptized into Christ's death and Resurrection (Rom 6:11) and because he was nourished on the Savior's flesh (1 Cor 10:16). It is this Baptism and this food that are the bond of the Christian fellowship.

When St. Paul received the gentiles into the Church, he emphasized that they had been saved by the mercy of God. Though the Jewish faith had once been true, its promise had been fulfilled in Christ. Therefore, Christians were no longer bound to circumcision nor to the keeping of the Jewish ceremonial taboos concerning washings and eating.

Salvation came as God's free gift. God's Ten Commandments were nothing more than the reiteration of the moral law found in the hearts of all men, pagans, Jews, and Christians. In themselves they had no power to save. They merely underlined man's sinfulness. To be a good human being, a man had to observe the Ten Commandments. But salvation, eternal life in and with Christ, came from faith and confidence in God's freely given promise.

Paul Fights the Judaizers

This new spirit of liberty from the old ceremonial laws shocked some converted Jews who wished to impose circumcision upon gentile converts. So fanatically did some of these Jewish converts cling to the old ways that even St. Peter hesitated to cross this Judaizing element among the early

Christians (Gal 1:11-14). This first great crisis in the history of the Church was settled at a council held in Jerusalem about the year 50 A.D. Under the leadership of Peter and of James, the bishop of Jerusalem, the council determined that Paul had taught correctly and that newly converted gentiles had only to believe and be baptized. They would observe the Ten Commandments as any good human being. But the day of ceremonial washings and circumcision as a religious mark was over (Acts 15).

St. Paul's vindication at the Council of Jerusalem in no way challenged the authority of St. Peter as the leader of the Church. Christ had selected Simon Peter as the rock upon which he intended to found his Church (Mt 16:13-20). At the Last Supper, our Lord had singled out Peter as the one apostle upon whom all the others could rely, for his faith would not fail him (Lk 22:31-34). And this he stated knowing full well that Peter would betray him three times that very day. Before his Ascension into heaven, Christ had called Peter the shepherd of his flock — a term he had previously used only in reference to himself — while the other apostles remained only his "little flock" (Jn 21:15-17; Lk 12:32; Mt 10:16 where as "sheep" they were sent into the midst of wolves). In this small Messianic community, where so many had actually seen the Lord, they knew how Christ had singled Peter out as leader. In this small Messianic community, where everyone knew each other by name, St. Peter's authority was taken for granted. There was no need to prove it. Even the fact that St. Paul boasts of "resisting him (Peter) to his face because he was in the wrong" (when Peter held aloof from the gentile converts of Paul to please the Jewish converts of Jerusalem) implies the importance of this man whom he resisted (Gal 2:11-14).

Paul Did Not Invent Christianity

Though Paul was probably the most effective apostle of Christianity, it must not be supposed that he invented the Church. Jesus Christ founded his Church. He selected Paul to be the apostle of the gentiles, the one who would take that Church to the pagan world. Paul, far from inventing the Church, had seen it as a ready-formed enemy of Judaism and had set out to destroy it. When God made known to him his destiny, he sacrificed a great deal to become a member of the organization he had wished to liquidate. In his Epistles, he emphasizes that he writes only what was passed on to him and what he had

19

previously taught his readers by word of mouth as an apostle of the Church of Jesus Christ.

It is also good to note that the Church of Christ was in existence several years before the first book of the New Testament was ever written. The Gospels and Epistles taught no new doctrine that the Church of Christ had not been constantly teaching orally before they had been penned. The Gospels and Epistles were written by Catholics, for Catholics, and within the Catholic Church. They were written to aid the Church in its mission, not to replace it. After the last of them was set down, the Church still continued to be the divinely constituted mouthpiece of God. It spoke in the name of Jesus Christ. As St. John put it, "He who knows God listens to us; he who is not of God does not listen to us" (1 Jn 4-6). In the ancient Church there was no conflict between the Bible and ecclesiastical authority. The Bible was God's word, and the Church, which he had founded, was his official interpreter.

Discussion Questions

1. Why did Jesus Christ gather a fellowship that would be known as the Church?
2. What is the Good News that Jesus brings?
3. Was a conflict between Jews and Christians inevitable?
4. Did Paul invent Christianity?
5. Why did Paul so strenuously fight the Judaizers? Was he anti-Semitic?

Chapter 2
Christians to the Lions! Why?

──────── Some of Christ's Fragile Fellowship ────────

Justin Martyr (c. 100-165) — Christian PR man.
Tertullian (c. 160-220) — the Christian "Philadelphia lawyer."
Augustine (354-430) — African Christian genius.
Irenaeus (c. 130-200) — Rome teaches what Christ taught.
Clement I (c. 96) — Rome commands peace in Corinth.
Cyprian of Carthage (d. 258) — the bishop who ran away to die another day.

The rapid spread of Christianity was surely due primarily to God who gives faith. However, there were numerous natural factors that made the middle of the 1st century the propitious time for "the hour of salvation."

Throughout the Roman Empire there were perhaps 5 million Jews. Many of these received the long-awaited Messiah, Jesus Christ, with joy. Because they had been zealous to make converts to their beliefs when they were still Jews, this same zeal animated their newly found faith. Christianity also attracted the so-called God-fearing pagans who were deeply interested in Judaism, but were reluctant to burden themselves with all the Jewish ceremonial laws. Prepared by the proselytizing of the Jews living outside of the Holy Land, these God-fearing gentiles came the more willingly to Christ.

Low Ebb of Roman Civilization

Despite the veneer of Greek culture that characterized the pagan world of the Roman Empire, public morality was at a very low ebb. Divorce destroyed family life among the upper classes. To keep the people quiet in the face of increasing state control, the various emperors and their local representatives sponsored public spectacles that appealed to the bestial elements of the mob. Gladiatorial combat contributed to the blood lust of the people. Theatrical productions catered to immorality. Around the year 113 A.D., Emperor Trajan staged a show for the Roman populace that lasted 117 days. He sent into mortal combat 4,941 pairs of gladiators. On the other hand, the theater emphasized the erotic and the brutal. Plays dealing with adultery, incest, even bestiality were acted out in horrid reality. Condemned criminals were often tortured to death on the stage of the amphitheater to make the tragedy of Prometheus more realistic.

Thirst for Salvation

Though the majority of the people were morbidly entranced by the games and public spectacles, many thinking people had long since become disgusted. The public cult of the mythological gods, encouraged by the government to maintain order, did not in any way foster morality or offer any hope in the face of death. After the death of Nero, emperor worship remained nothing but a patriotic function. The serious minded, in desperation, turned to private religions coming out of Egypt and Persia. They worshiped Osiris or Mithras because these deities promised some sort of immortality, and because their cult demanded some degree of self-denial and good works in order to merit the help of the god.

Those inclined to philosophy could follow the grim Stoics who taught detachment from all worldly things in the face of a doom that was inevitable. Platonism, in varying forms, also preached self-denial of material things so that a man could more closely unite himself to the spiritual source of all good. Reaction against public immorality and brutality, as well as a concern for salvation after death, made many pagans glad to receive the Good News of Christ when they heard it.

Why Nero Picked on the Christians

In general, Rome was very tolerant of the different religious beliefs of her subjects. She especially protected the religion of the Jews. Since, in official eyes, there was little distinction between Christianity and Judaism, the followers of Christ profited from their Jewish background. According to St. Irenaeus (c. 200), St. Peter and St. Paul had founded the Christian community in Rome itself. Though not particularly liked by the pagans, who found them too stand-offish and secretive, the Christians managed to live in peace until the burning of Rome by Nero in the year 64 A.D. To save himself from the anger of the mob, Nero blamed the Christians for the fire. A handful were rounded up by the police. Confessions and accusations that involved coreligionists were obtained by means of torture. To turn the tragedy of a burned city into a "spectacular" worthy of his brutal subjects, Nero had the Christians crucified in the circus that stood where the Vatican gardens now stand. In order to light the festivities of the evening, the emperor had the crucified Christians covered with pitch and ignited as human torches. It was during Nero's persecution that both St. Peter (between 64-68) and St. Paul (68) laid down their lives for Christ.

"Lynch Law" Persecution

To legalize the persecution of the Christians, Nero decreed that no one could profess this belief. Though a whispering campaign carried on by the pagans had accused them of everything from atheism to cannibalism, Christians were hunted out, up until the 3rd century, simply because they professed a proscribed religion. In the 3rd century, the Christians were often accused of treason because they refused to burn incense to the emperor as a form of worship. However, it must also be remembered that legal distinctions often carried little weight with a pagan mob in Rome or Antioch or Smyrna. Many Christians died the victims of "lynch law," with little or no semblance of a trial.

Though it seems quite probable that Christian martyrs may be numbered in the millions, nevertheless, they were not continually under fire between the years of Nero and the Edict of Toleration of 313. At times, the persecution abated, and there were times during this period when the followers of Christ were not persecuted at all. During the reign of Trajan, Pliny the Younger, the governor of Bythinia (c. 100) asked the emperor for a policy to follow in the prosecution of Christians. Trajan replied that the governor ought not to initiate a search for Christians, but, if one was denounced, he should be induced to give up his belief. If the Christian refused, he was to be condemned. In general, the Roman government followed this official policy, but this did not save the Christians from the malice of the local populace anxious to hunt them out.

Why the Pagans Hated the Christians

When we think of the Roman persecutions, we often think of the Church underground, hiding from the light in endless stretches of catacombs that honeycomb the foundations of the imperial city. This is, of course, to localize too greatly the extent of the Church's suffering. For her martyrs shed their blood not only in Italy but in Asia Minor, Africa, and as far west as Narbonne and Lyons in Gaul. While the Roman catacombs were surely used as burial places and as refuges from time to time, in general, Christians met for the breaking of bread, the Mass, in their own homes.

The persecution of Christians waxed when a plague struck Rome or when the barbarians broke through the defense line along the Danube, for the so-called impiety of the followers of Christ, who refused to worship pagan gods, was usually blamed for such catastrophes. But, by the beginning of the 3rd century, the very number of the Christians made it clear that the policy of persecution was failing. The Asiatic proconsul, Arius Antoninus, found so many Christians in his custody that he was forced to release most of them with a contemptuous, "You fools, if you want to die, don't you have enough rope and cliffs?"

An insidious literary campaign that constantly accused the Christians of being atheists, immoral, and unpatriotic was answered by such authors as Aristides of Athens, St. Justin Martyr, and Tertullian. In their defense of their faith, they helped to found a school of Christian literature that would reach its glory in the works of St. Augustine of Hippo.

Discord in the Early Church

If the Church of the first three centuries was besieged from without by pagan persecution, she also had to contend with discord within the ranks.

First of all, the persecutions became a divisive force within the Church. There were Christians who were less than heroic in the face of threatened torture and death. To save their lives, they denied their faith or compromised it. Very often, when a persecution subsided, these individuals would seek to return to the Church. The question would inevitably arise concerning the penance they were to do to make up for their betrayal of the faith. Some bishops were overly severe, others not severe enough. Factions either for or against the penitent divided — even to the point of bloodshed — many Christian communities.

Gnosticism was a religious philosophy older than Christianity, but it came out in a Christian edition as well. Claiming to give a secret knowledge (*gnosis* in Greek) exclusively to those who joined in one of its many sects, Gnosticism, in general,

24

taught that God was otherwise beyond the reach of any human mind. Certain Gnostics denied that Christ really had a body, and others claimed that the God of the Old Testament made all material things which were evil, while the God of the New Testament made all spiritual things which were good. Such mysterious teaching was dangerous, for it could obscure the clearly stated Good News of Christ. To combat this *gnosis*, Christian writers like St. Paul, St. John, and St. Irenaeus insisted upon holding fast to the traditional teaching of the Church.

Among the Christian lunatic fringe were the millenarians and the Montanists. Both believed that the end of the world was at hand and that Christ's second coming was imminent. Montanus, who founded Montanism, believed that he was the Paraclete sent by Christ to clarify the teachings of Christianity. Many Christians were influenced by millenarian teaching, eagerly awaiting the 1,000 years of peace upon this earth that would follow upon Christ's Second Coming. The Montanists could boast that they had converted the great Christian writer, Tertullian, to their cause.

In the 3rd century, certain heretics denied that Christ was really God, equal to the Father. Paul of Samosata, bishop of Antioch (c. 290), seemed to put Jesus on a par with Moses and the prophets, a man selected to reveal God's mind to us.

Once again, Christian literature was enriched by the great writers who combated these heresies — men of the stamp of Clement of Alexandria (c. 200), Origen (253), and Tertullian before he fell to the Montanists. Though controversy within the Church weakened its unity, it served also as an occasion to think out, clarify, and accurately explain the truths of Christ's teaching.

Life in the Early Church

Despite persecution and doctrinal wrangling, the life of the Church developed. Converts, after lengthy instruction, were baptized, usually by immersion in a river (*Didache*, 7). The ceremony of the breaking of bread, the Mass, bound the Christian community together in the real flesh and blood of Jesus Christ (1 Cor 11:17-34; Ignatius of Antioch, *Ad Smyrn*, 6; Justin Martyr, *I Apol*, chapter 65). Though the baptized Christian was a man who had abandoned his pagan life to take upon himself the life of Jesus Christ, he could sin. If he did, these sins could be forgiven after Baptism provided that he did penance and was firmly resolved to follow Christ once again (*Shepherd*

25

of Hermas, Mand., 4, 3, 6).

Everywhere, bishops who received their power to rule from the apostles (Clement of Rome, 1 Cor 44:1-3) offered sacrifice and directed the Church in their particular locality (Ignatius of Antioch, *Ad Smyrn,* 8, 9). If the Christian community was large enough to warrant it, the bishop would ordain presbyters to assist him in the functions of the liturgy. Deacons, besides instructing, saw to the various charities of the Church and distributed the Eucharist.

Rome, the Rock of the Church

Just as Christ selected Peter as the rock upon which his Church would stand, so the bishops who succeeded Peter continued to enjoy universal authority in the Church. The other bishops, successors of the apostles, were responsible for their own sees. Though the government of the Church was not as strongly centralized as it is today, the primacy of Rome — the See of Peter — was taken for granted. This is clear from the way the successors of Peter acted and from the respect that was accorded the Roman See.

Around the year 96 A.D., Pope Clement I authoritatively demanded the settlement of a dispute that rocked the Church at Corinth (Clement of Rome, 1 Cor 59:1). It is interesting to note that Clement exercized his power at a time when St. John, the beloved of the Lord, was still alive, implying that the authority of the See of Peter surpassed even that of an apostle.

According to St. Irenaeus (c. 130-200), if a local bishop teaches what is taught by the bishop of Rome, he is surely teaching the faith of Christ. For the bishops of the Roman See can easily trace their spiritual lineage back to the apostles, Peter and Paul, and they have kept faithfully the tradition of Christ (St. Irenaeus, *Contra Haereses,* III, chapter III, 1-4).

St. Ignatius of Antioch, by his special deference to the Roman See, seems to imply its special authority in the Church (St. Ignatius, *Ad. Rom.,* Prologue, 4:3; 9:1).

When the Church at Lyons (Gaul) asked the aid of the bishop of Rome in its battle against the Montanists, a judgment was sent immediately.

Pope Victor I (190-198) settled upon the exact manner of calculating the date of Easter after this controversy had divided the Church for many years. Those who failed to accept his decision found themselves excommunicated from the Church, no matter in what diocese they lived. Here was a case of an ecclesiastical issue settled for the whole Church by the bishop of Rome.

Another telling indication of the special authority of the Roman See is the fact that heretics, posing as true Christians, passed up older sees, such as Jerusalem, Antioch, Ephesus, or Corinth, and appealed to Rome for a decision which they hoped would favor their cause.

Toleration of Christianity

Toward the end of his reign, in 303, Diocletian, influenced no doubt by his caesar, Galerius, unleashed perhaps the most frightful persecution that the Church had ever suffered. Thousands of Christians in Asia Minor, Africa, and Greece were mutilated or put to the sword. However, by 311, Galerius, who had succeeded Diocletian, had to admit defeat. Grudgingly he granted full liberty to Christians to believe and worship as they wished; should their God be the true God, as they claimed, it was their duty to gain his favor for the Roman Empire, so reasoned Galerius. Unfortunately he died before enacting his decree and his successor in the East, Maxim Daia, carried on the persecution. In 312, at the battle of the Milvian Bridge, the western emperor, Constantine, went through some sort of religious experience, and he marked the shields of his soldiers with Chi-Rho, the Greek monogram of Christ. He successfully defeated his rival, Maxentius, and in 313 decreed the edict of Milan, granting general religious toleration in the empire. At long last, Christianity was permitted to live above ground.

Discussion Questions

1. Why was the middle of the 1st century propitious for "the hour of salvation"?

2. Compare Roman reasons for persecuting the Church with those of the Communists today.

3. Discuss the role that Galerius' decree of tolerance gave to Christians in the empire.

4. Discuss the danger of Gnosticism forming a Church within the Church. Are there such parallel dangers today?

5. Discuss indications of Roman primacy in the first two centuries of the Church's existence.

Chapter 3
The Early Christian Empire

—————————Some of Christ's Fragile Fellowship —————

Constantine (274 or 288-337) — the Roman emperor who gave the Church the keys to the city.
Constantine II — thought religion too important to leave to the Church.
John Chrysostom (c. 347-407) — fought "city hall" and lost.
Leo I (d. 461) — the pope who put Constantinople in its place.
Arius (c. 250-336) — was Christ God?
Eutyches (c. 378-454) — scandalized at Christ's humanity.
Martin of Tours (d. 387) — monks in the West.

Though the edict of Milan was phrased in such a way as to avoid favoring any particular religion, Christianity actually profited the most. The followers of Christ composed sizable communities in practically every city of the empire. The decree of Constantine restored to these communities any Church property that had been confiscated during the persecutions. The government gave subsidies for the building and beautifying of churches. In Rome the Lateran Palace became the pope's residence and the Lateran Basilica rose above the tomb of St. Peter. In 324 Constantine began the splendid basilicas that graced Bethlehem and Mt. Calvary in the Holy Land.

Constantine did not receive Baptism until on his deathbed, but much of his legislation reflected the Christian spirit. Christian churches were granted the right of sanctuary, and bishops enjoyed a rising prestige in the empire. They could administer Church properties and could even wield civil jurisdiction over their clergy. By the end of the 4th century, clerics were exempted from civil taxation.

Christianity Becomes the Religion of the Empire

Nevertheless, in the 4th century the vast majority of imperial subjects were still pagans. Emperor Constantine continued to function as *pontifex maximus* (imperial high priest) in the liturgical services of the Roman state cults. However, the persecution of Christianity had done nothing to make the old pagan myths any more credible. In the cities of the empire, paganism was actually in its death throes. Even the highly effective methods of Emperor Julian (361-363) to restore the old religion proved fruitless. By the middle of the 4th century Emperor Constantius had ordered the pagan temples closed and had forbidden idolatry. Gratian (375-383) withdrew state aid from the priestly colleges and the vestal virgins, and he renounced the title of *pontifex maximus*. In 392 Emperor Theodosius I (379-395) banned all public and private sacrifices to the gods. Christianity became the official religion of the Roman Empire. However, paganism in the superstitious rural areas of the West was slow in dying, and many generations passed before the old cults disappeared entirely.

How the Emperors Ran Religion

If Christianity benefited by the protection, and finally the adoption, of the Roman Empire, it also suffered at the hands of most emperors, who could never forget that each had once been *pontifex maximus*. They were sincerely concerned that God be worshiped properly in order to placate him and win his protection of the empire. Supreme rulers in the civilized world, the emperors, almost of necessity, intervened in the affairs of the Church. Ecumenical councils were convoked by the emperor and, when the bishops traveled to them, they were sped on their way by imperial troops. At times the theological penchants of an emperor could go so far as to impose doctrine upon the Christian people, as in the case of Arianism protected and fostered by Emperor Constantius II. If a man like St. Ambrose of Milan cried out against this caesaropapism — reminding Theodosius I that palaces, not churches, were the emperor's concern — St. Augustine, in North Africa, could urge the use of the "secular arm" in combating fanatical Donatism. St. John Chrysostom died in exile because he had criticized the frivolity of Empress Eudoxia.

The totalitarian attitudes of certain Byzantine emperors of the 6th and 7th centuries led them into prolonged and even bloody controversy with the Church and those loyal to true doctrine. Churchmen, living in the emperor's court at Constantinople, inevitably were more impressed with imperial domination than were the popes and bishops of the West. But until the founding of the holy Roman Empire of the West in the 9th century, no one was safe from the emperors' ecclesiastical tyranny. Most emperors thought, as did Justinian II (687), that they were "by divine mercy appointed guardians of the faith." Nor was this idea to be limited to the emperors of Constantinople. History seems to show that wherever the Church has had to live in an authoritarian state, no government has been able to resist the temptation to interfere in her affairs.

Church Follows Empire

The Church was organized along the lines of civil authority within the Roman Empire. Every city had a bishop, often elected by the people, who enjoyed a sovereign power to teach, ordain, judge his clergy, and administer Church property. He could not interfere in the affairs of another see, nor could he change sees. Ordinarily, he was wedded to his see for life. As Roman civil authority fell into decay, especially in cities along the empire's northern and western frontiers, the bishop took on more prestige than the town's magistrates.

Above the level of cities, the empire was divided into provinces. The Church also followed this division. Ordinarily, the bishop who ruled in the provincial capital also exercised a certain authority over the bishops of the cities and towns within the province. Called the metropolitan, it was his duty to officiate at the consecration of any bishops of his province, and twice a year he assembled his suffragan bishops to judge appeals that came from individual episcopal courts.

From the beginning of the 4th century, when the capital of the empire was changed from Rome to Constantinople, the empire was divided into ethnical groupings called dioceses. These dioceses were later to become the independent kingdoms of France, Spain, and Britain, to mention only a few. The Church followed this division by putting a patriarch or primate at the head of each imperial diocese. In Italy, the patriarch was, of course, the pope; in Africa, it was the bishop of Carthage. By the 5th century, the patriarchs of Constantinople, Alexandria, Antioch, and Jerusalem ruled the metropolitans and bishops of their respective dioceses under the supreme authority of the pope of Rome.

The Importance of the Apostolic See

Always honored in a special way as the "Apostolic See" (so named by the end of the 4th century), we have already seen indications of the supremacy of Roman ecclesiastical authority during the first three centuries of the Church's troubled existence. The pope's jurisdiction over all the episcopal sees of the West was proclaimed by the Council of Sardica in 343. This written declaration reflects a tradition that had been taken for granted up until that time. The Roman council of 378 placed all metropolitans under the immediate jurisdiction of the Apostolic See. The popes of the 4th century acted upon this authority by settling, through rulings and decretals, doctrinal and disciplinary disputes in Africa, Gaul, and Spain.

The patriarchs of Constantinople, conscious of their dignity as bishops of the new Roman capital, were anxious to enhance their power over less influential sees. To safeguard their position against more ancient sees, such as Antioch, Alexandria, or Jerusalem, the Fathers of the first Council of Constantinople (381) and at the Council of Chalcedon (451) claimed for the "new Rome" the second place in the Church, second only to the old Rome. Though this claim was not made as a challenge to Roman primacy, it was still not acceptable to the Apostolic See and was rejected. Even though the Church had followed the political divisions of the empire in determining her own organization, nevertheless, the dignity of an episcopal see, according to Pope Leo the Great (451), was established by her apostolic origin and antiquity. No apostle had founded Constantinople, and the "new Rome" was a Johnny-come-lately to Christianity.

To enable the bishops to more effectively rule the Church in a province or in a diocese, a council could be called. Where a problem was of more universal importance, the emperor could convoke an ecumenical or general council. To this council would come a large number of the bishops of the empire. The pope, either in person or through his legates, would preside, though his presence was not of the essence. The decrees of an ecumenical council bound the entire Church if approved by the pope.

The Crucible of Theological Speculation

Freed from the constant anxiety of persecution, Christians had the leisure to ponder over the truths of God's revelation made through Jesus Christ. Eastern Catholics, given to theological speculation (the heritage of Hellenism), endeavored to explain the nature of God and his Word, Jesus Christ. Well-intentioned and talented as many of these thinkers were, their theories often led to theological error.

In the first quarter of the 4th century, Arius, a priest of Alexandria, taught that the Word was only an adopted son of God and therefore not divine. Condemned by the Council of Nicaea in 325, certain followers of Arius were influential enough to gain the ear of several emperors. Constantius II and Valens attempted to impose Arianism upon the empire and succeeded quite well in the East. The stout opposition of St. Athanasius of Alexandria, championed by Rome, and the conciliatory work of St. Gregory of Nyssa and St. Basil prepared the way for a final condemnation of Arianism at the first Council of Constantinople (381).

Nestorius, the patriarch of Constantinople, taught that there were two persons in Jesus Christ — one divine, the other merely human. The Blessed Virgin Mary gave birth to the human being and therefore could not be called the Mother of God. St. Cyril of Alexandria, using every means in his power, had this dangerous doctrine condemned at the Council of Ephesus (431).

Going to the opposite extreme, Eutyches, the grand abbot of the monks of Constantinople, began to preach that Christ's human nature was absorbed into his divine nature "like a drop of honey in the water of the sea." This doctrine, Monophysitism, denied that Christ was really a human being and Pope Leo I strongly condemned it at the Council of Chalcedon (451).

From the 5th to the 7th century, the East was torn in controversy over the issue of Monophysitism. This religious crisis continued because certain emperors either positively favored the teaching of Eutyches or certain forms of it, or because they were afraid to condemn it outrightly for fear of raising civil war. Besieged from without by the Persians in the East and the barbarian Germanic tribes along the northern frontier, emperors like Zeno attempted to impose theological compromises that were acceptable to no orthodox Christian. Men like St. Maximus and Pope St. Martin I paid with their lives for their unwillingness to conform to the imperial decrees. At length, in 681, at the second Council of Constantinople, the great controversies over the kind of being Jesus Christ was came to an end by adopting the teaching of the Roman pontiffs since the time of Leo the Great: Jesus Christ is a divine person subsisting in two distinct natures — one human, the other divine.

Battle over Practice in the West

In the West, theological controversy was on a more practical level. The Donatists of Africa believed that sacraments depended upon the worthiness of the one who conferred them for their supernatural power. They attempted to set up a Puritan-like Church that excluded sinners and rebaptized any converts coming to them from the Catholic Church. When they gathered a large following in Africa, Donatism was condemned by the Council of Arles (314). Following the practice of the Roman See, the council condemned the rebaptism of validly baptized Christians and pioneered the teaching that sacraments give the grace they signify independently of the worthiness of the person who confers them. However, the Donatists were still a power to be coped with in the 5th century, and St. Augustine championed orthodoxy against them.

At the beginning of the 5th century, Pelagius, a priest from Britain, in defending man's free will and his obligation to strive for sanctity, denied original sin and the practical need for divine grace. Because of his personal virtue and his powerful preaching, Pelagius made followers in Rome and in North Africa. St. Augustine, proving man's fall and absolute need of God's grace from the writings of St. Paul, led the fight against Pelagius' followers.

How Christians Worshiped

Despite doctrinal conflicts, the Church continued to offer sacrifice to God and to bestow the sacraments. The celebrant of the Mass was usually the bishop, but, as early as the time of St. Ignatius of Antioch (c. 110), bishops had begun to ordain presbyters who assisted them in the liturgy. These presbyters often lived in common with their bishop, and by the 4th century they were vowed to celibacy in the Western Church.

Sunday Mass was the center of Christian worship, and by the 2nd century the ceremonies surrounding it varied with the locality. The Greek language prevailed in the East and remained the official liturgical tongue of Rome itself until the 3rd century. Though the Mass was celebrated in several different rites, the different liturgies resembled each other. The faithful received Holy Communion ordinarily under both species, taking the small leavened Eucharistic roll in their hands and sipping the sacred blood from the chalice with a straw. After the Sunday sermon, the bishop said Mass at a table without cross, candles, or tabernacle. He celebrated the Holy Sacrifice facing the people. The service took several hours, mainly because of the lengthy sermons; on one occasion they say that Hilary of Arles (5th century) spoke as long as 4 hours.

Christian Saints and Sinners

During the 1st century, special honors were paid to martyrs who followed Christ in his Passion. With the persecutions ended, those who confessed their faith by a pious life became objects of devotion, and their feast days were kept. The Blessed Virgin Mary was especially honored as God's Mother, and the defeat of Nestorius at Ephesus (431) increased this devotion in the Eastern Church.

The end of the persecutions made it difficult to die for Christ, but there were many Christians who renounced the world and withdrew into the deserts of Egypt and Syria to live for Christ alone. However, living alone often proved spiritually dangerous. In the 4th century, St. Pachomius organized the first monastic communities in the Egyptian desert. His monks lived an austere life of prayer and penance, and they were ruled by an abbot or father. St. Basil the Great was the lawgiver of Eastern monasticism. In the West, St. Martin of Tours founded Marmoutier in 371 and became the father of Western monasticism.

Not all Christians were saints in these early centuries. Those who committed grave public sins were made to do difficult and humiliating penances. For certain very grave sins, they might receive absolution only on their deathbed. From about the 5th century, private penance for secret offenses coexisted with the public form.

Discussion Questions

1. Compare Christ's fellowship in the empire of Constantine with its status in the beginning.

2. Why were the Christian Roman emperors so anxious to govern the Church?

3. Discuss how the God-man, Jesus Christ, became a scandal to certain Christians such as Arius, Nestorius, and Eutyches.

4. Why was the Donatist concept, a Church without sinners, unacceptable to Christ's fragile fellowship?

5. Through additional investigation, compare the Mass liturgy of the ancient Church with the liturgy of your parish.

Chapter 4
The Conversion of the Barbarians

At the beginning of the 5th century, a dire event occurred in Western Europe. The barbarians overran the empire's northern and western frontiers. In 406 the Germans stormed Trier's Porta Nigra, and they crossed the Rhine to pour into Gaul. In the year 410 the impossible happened: Alaric, the Vandal, took Rome.

A contemporary American can hope to understand the effects of these disasters upon Roman civilization in the West if he attempts to imagine what the consequences of a successful atomic bombing of America's 10 largest cities would be for American civilization. These savages of the Teutonic North made the Gallo-Roman Christians of the 5th century, not to mention the simple Jewish folk of Christ's time, paragons of sophistication by comparison. The barbarian hordes all but buried Greco-Roman culture in the Western world.

Christians, who were loyal to the empire as the only safeguard of their faith and civilization, resisted the invaders. In the defense of the cities of Gaul, the bishops often took the lead, since the weak imperial government in Ravenna and far-off Constantinople proved helpless before the invaders. Because of the selfless leadership of bishops like Exuperius of Toulouse and Nicasius of Rheims, not to mention the valiant Germaine of Auxerre, the prestige of the Church increased. When the last Roman emperor of the West was no more, at the end of the 5th

century, the only vestige of the empire that remained in the West was the Catholic faith of its citizens. As the barbarians began to settle in Gaul — the Franks to the North, the Burgundians and Vandals to the South — they treated with the bishops of the Gallo-Roman cities as the only civil authorities that remained.

Barbarians Become Roman Catholic

Though, at first, Roman Christians were reluctant to have anything to do with their barbarian conquerors, by the beginning of the 6th century they came to realize that they must convert and civilize the Western empire's new overlords. There seems to have been little systematic planning for the conversion of the barbarians, though the papacy attempted to coordinate missionary activities, especially in the last years of the 6th century.

In the South, the Visigoths and Vandals, Germanic people who were also Arians, settled in areas that were largely Catholic. Because Arianism, with its virtual denial of Christ's divinity, sapped their Christianity of strength, they became candidates for orthodox Catholicism. During the 6th century, thanks to

cared nothing for the lot of the poor. It was the official task of the Church to feed the hungry, clothe the naked, nurse the sick and the old, and safeguard the rights of serfs and prisoners.

The Church As the Spirit of Rome

In a world that was essentially rural, a large monastery became a center of civilization. Here and in the schools sponsored by the cathedrals, the tradition of Western culture was to be passed on to young scholars. Though the classical authors were read, the liberal arts course gradually was made a preparation for the study of theology and Scripture. What remained of Roman art and architecture was Christianized. Ancient public baths were often turned into baptistries and the design of Roman housing supplied the lines of the basilica-styled church.

From the 5th through the 8th century, the world of the West was snatched from the power of Roman political authority. If the light of Roman cultural tradition was not snuffed out by the icy blast of the barbarian North, it was because these barbarians valued Roman culture, and because the Church of Rome, the only existing vestige of that culture, converted its conquerors and passed on to them most of the things of value that Roman civilization had to offer.

Discussion Questions

1. Discuss the initial attitude of Roman Catholics toward their barbarian conquerors in the West. Are there any equivalent attitudes today among Roman Catholics?
2. Compare the two monastic spirits, Celtic and Benedictine, that converted the barbarians of the West.
3. How did the monks of St. Benedict unify the Church in the West?
4. Discuss the missionary tactics of the monks among the barbarians. How did these tactics influence the teaching methods of the Church through the centuries?
5. Compare the mission of a monastery in the early Middle Ages with that of a parish community today.

Chapter 5
How Charlemagne Shaped
a New Roman Empire

———————— Some of Christ's Fragile Fellowship ————————

Justinian I (482-565) — tried to get back the Roman Empire's lost real estate in the West.

Pepin the Short (c. 714-768) — Boniface's Old Testament king.

Charlemagne (c. 742-814) — "king and priest, leader and guide of all the Christian people."

Alcuin (735-804) — Charlemagne's English schoolmaster.

Pope Leo III (d. 816) — Charlemagne's Roman Moses.

Irene (752-803) — blinded her son to be empress of Constantinople and lost the West to the Franks.

The establishment of an independent empire in the West divided Christendom in two. For centuries there had been only one Roman Empire. Though it may have been ruled by a team of emperors at times, its laws bound both the East and the West, and up until the 5th century they could be enforced. With the barbarian inroads of the 5th century, this was no longer possible in the West. The crowning of Charlemagne on Christmas day, 800, as the new holy Roman emperor of the West (while an Eastern Roman empress reigned in Constantinople) corresponded to the reality of the situation: There was a new world in the West that the old Roman Empire could no longer control. The survival of what remained of Roman civilization depended upon law and order. Since Constantinople could no longer guarantee this, another imperial power had to be found that could.

By the end of the 5th century, the Roman Empire no longer controlled the Balkans nor Italy, not to mention the Iberian Peninsula or Gaul. Despite the desperate and successful efforts of Justinian I (reigned 527-565) to restore Roman rule in North Africa, parts of Spain, Gaul, and Italy, his work was of no lasting value. By the end of the 7th century, North Africa had fallen into Mohammedan hands. In 568 the Lombards invaded Italy and set up principalities in the North and center, though a strip of territory from Ravenna to Rome and points south remained in imperial hands. In order to carry on his campaign in the West against the barbarians, Justinian had bribed the empire's traditional enemy, the Persians, with tribute to secure the Eastern frontier. Though Justinian was the last Roman emperor to singly rule a territory anywhere near as large as that of Trajan, all was not well within the gates. The restoration was an effort too great for the empire's financial resources. Its grip on the newly reconquered lands was always weak, for there were provinces like Egypt and Syria that yearned for national independence and were quite willing to betray the empire to get it.

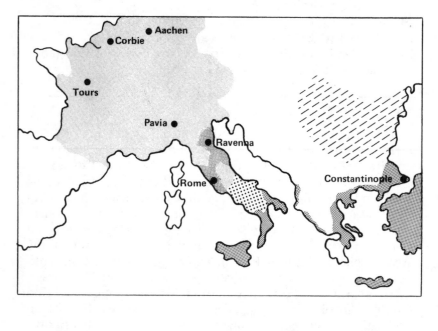

Bulgar territory	Borders of Charlemagne's empire	Lombard territory	Byzantine empire	Patrimony of St. Peter

The Old Roman Empire Under Siege

After Justinian's death, Emperor Maurice attempted to protect his subjects against the inroads of the barbarian Avars and Slavs, who were plundering the empire along the Danubian frontier. To carry on this campaign, Maurice had inherited an empty treasury. He was therefore forced to, at least temporarily, withdraw troops from Italy and the Balkans. Once again the Persians were bribed to keep them from going on the rampage. When Maurice was killed by his own soldiers, Constantinople fell into chaotic civil strife for some 8 years (602-610). This gave the Persian Emperor Chosroes II ample time to ravage Syria, Palestine, and Asia Minor at will.

It was the genius of Heraclius that saved the Roman Empire from falling to the Persians. Dividing the East into military districts, called themes, he put over each a military governor and planted them with citizen soldiers who would defend them because they had a stake in the land that was given to them to cultivate. In 629 Heraclius' day of triumph came, for in that year he carried the true Cross, which the Persians had seized in 614, through the gates of the city of Jerusalem.

But once again the military victories of the Roman Empire were short-lived. Before it could recoup the expenses in men and money that the campaign against the Persians had cost, a new and fanatically aggressive enemy had arisen to challenge the empire.

The prophet Mohammed died in 632. But his Arab followers, fanatically devoted and spurred on by a lust for plunder, carried his religious beliefs, a mixture of myth, Christianity, and Judaism, into the Near East in a matter of years. Throughout the rest of the century, they pushed their conquests into Egypt, North Africa, and Spain. By 678 the Mohammedans were able to blockade Constantinople itself. Though the battle of Tours, 732, determined that they would not sweep into Gaul, more than half the Roman Empire now remained in Mohammedan hands.

The Lombards Take the Italian Peninsula

When the Lombard tribes invaded Northern Italy in the second half of the 6th century, though the Romans tried to resist, they were no match for these Arian Germans from the Elbe. Constantinople, hard pressed by the Bulgars and Avars to the north, and the Persians to the south and east, could do nothing to aid the beleaguered West. The Lombards occupied Milan and Pavia, and threatened the headquarters of the emperor's viceroy, the exarch, at Ravenna. Thanks largely to the resistance of the popes, the Lombards were not able to take the territories of the papacy (territories loyal to the Roman Empire). This patrimony of St. Peter, as it was called, girded Italy with a diagonal Roman belt, for south of it certain Lombard dukes had seized land well into Calabria. The rest of the South remained, at this date, in imperial hands.

Though the initial invasions were raids that bathed Italy in bloody murder, arson, and rape, the Lombards eventually settled in several duchies and absorbed the religion and culture of their Roman subjects — those who survived. By the middle of the 8th century, the Lombard invaders spoke and dressed like Romans. In fact, the various independent Lombard dukes became respectable Catholics, vying with each other in donating land to the Church.

Why the Popes Remained Loyal to the Empire

Despite their open-handed Catholicism, the various popes of the 7th and 8th centuries resisted any attempt on the part of the Lombards to seize the imperial papal territory that girded the center of Italy. It is not easy to explain the papal attitude. In the 6th and 7th centuries, several popes had been bullied by the Roman emperors, and Martin I had been dragged off to exile and death. Through a good part of the 8th century, the papacy was at war with the iconoclastic (image-breaking) Roman emperors who opposed the use and veneration of pictures of our Lord, our Lady, and the saints. Nevertheless, it must be remembered that many popes of this period were of Greek origin and were notably subservient to the emperor. They also believed that it was their duty to preserve what they could of the Roman Empire. The Catholic Lombard kings would not, perhaps, have been more tyrannical than the emperors, but they were not Romans and had no right to imperial territory. It is also quite probable that, as imperial power lost its grip upon Italy, the popes had little desire to replace it with a Lombard king who might make Rome his capital and then totally dominate the Church.

In 751, Aistulf, the Lombard king of Pavia, seized Ravenna and decided to unite all of Italy under his rule. Pope Stephen II firmly opposed him. In 753 the pope went to Pavia as the personal representative of the Emperor Constantine V. He sought the restoration of the newly conquered imperial territory. When Aistulf refused and again threatened the lands of St. Peter, the pope crossed the Alps to beg the Catholic Franks to protect the Holy See from the threatened invasion.

Pepin and the Papal States

It was to Pepin the Short, the son of Charles Martel, who had stopped the Mohammedans at Tours (732), that Pope Stephen made his appeal. Proclaimed king of the Franks in 751, Pepin came from a line of rulers who had governed behind the scenes for the do-nothing Merovingian kings, and who, under Pepin of Herstal, had finally replaced them (c. 687) in fact, if not in law. To secure his hold upon the throne, Pepin, following the Jewish kings of the Old Testament, had had himself anointed by St. Boniface, the apostle of Gaul and Germany. This had given his kingly office a sacred prestige that not even royal blood could equal. Pope Stephen enhanced his status by once again anointing him and by naming him Patrician of the Romans. Armed with his new authority as protector of the Holy See, Pepin marched off to do battle with the Lombards and defeated them. In 756 he forced Aistulf to restore the imperial territories that he had seized, not to the emperor of Constantinople but to the pope. In this way, the Franks recognized the temporal kingdom of the popes, the Papal States, a sovereignty independent of the Roman Empire. Straddling the center of the Italian Peninsula, the Papal States secured the political independence of the popes, became a bone of contention to be toyed with and worried by ambitious Northern emperors, and stood as an obstacle to Italian unity until 1870.

Charlemagne Creates a Roman Catholic Empire

When Charlemagne, who gives his name to the Carolingian dynasty of Frankish kings, inherited his father's throne in 768, he fell into an imperial-sized kingdom. Charlemagne, anointed like his father, looked upon himself as "king and priest, leader and guide of all the Christian people." Threatened once again by the Lombards in 774, it was the great King Charles who defended the Papal States and, in fact, added more territory to them. But what he gave, he also closely watched, claiming his right as Patrician of the Romans to supervise political administration.

From approximately 771-804, Charles carried on a military campaign of unequaled ferocity against the pagan Saxons who had refused to become absorbed within the Frankish Empire. As a Christian, Charles was sincere in his desire to spread his religion. But he also saw it as a means of unifying the various ethnic groups within his kingdom — Goths, Lombards, Romans, Franks, and Slavs. Though his English mentor, Alcuin, discreetly opposed him, Charles forced his Saxon subjects into the Christian camp by imposing the death penalty for any pagan practices. In 782 he massacred 4,800 pagan Saxons, not so much for their heathenism, but because they had revolted against Frankish rule.

However, besides force, Charles relied upon monasteries and parish churches to develop Christianity within his realm. He founded episcopal sees at Münster, Osnabruck, Minden, and Bremen, to mention only a few. The famed monastery of Corbie opened its gates to Saxons who wished to follow Christ more closely. Though Charlemagne's campaign against the Saxons was cruel, it was effective and not without fruit. For, in the 10th century, long after the last of the Carolingian monarchs was dead and gone, it was to be a Saxon leader who would restore the Holy Roman Empire of the West.

In other military campaigns Charles expanded his realm from the English Channel to Trieste, from the Elbe River to the Pyrenees. By the beginning of the 9th century, he was really the successor of the old Roman emperors in the West. And when Charles looked toward Constantinople to find not only a usurper but a woman upon the imperial throne, the desire to assert his own imperial dignity as a matter of right, as well as fact, was overpowering.

The Crowning of Charlemagne

In November 800, Charles arrived in Rome to hold an inquiry into the conduct of Pope Leo III who had been accused by certain Romans of adultery and perjury. The emperor exonerated the pope of all charges after Leo solemnly swore that they were not true.

On Christmas day, 800, Charles prostrated himself before the tomb of St. Peter in the basilica. When he rose to get ready to hear Christmas Mass, Pope Leo approached him and placed a crown upon his head. On cue, the crowds in the basilica chanted their praises and begged Christ's protection of Charles. Then they cried three times, "Long life and victory to Charles, the pious Augustus, crowned by God, the great and peace-loving emperor of the Romans!" This ceremony was a pat imitation of an imperial coronation in Constantinople. After the crowning, the pope genuflected before the emperor as an act of veneration.

Following Charlemagne's official biographer, Eginhard, some historians claim that the emperor was taken by surprise and received the imperial crown unwillingly. That the crowning was a spontaneous affair seems highly improbable. The cast, including the emperor himself, knew their lines too well. It seems quite probable that, on the advice of Leo III, Charles decided to accept the imperial crown, since there was no one to protest save a usurping woman on the throne of Constantinople.

Because the pope crowned Charles in no way implied the supremacy of papal power over that of the emperor. Popes like Gregory VII and Innocent III, who had their troubles with the Western emperors, liked to underline this implication. However, they conveniently forgot that, just like the patriarch of Constantinople who crowned and anointed the Eastern emperor, Pope Leo III also "adored," by a genuflection, the imperial political power of Charlemagne. Coronation at the hands of the Church was merely the hallmark of God's blessing on his anointed.

The Catholic Faith Was the Blood of the Empire

Charlemagne made good use of churchmen in his empire. At the head of his chancery, which prepared and stored all official documents, was the emperor's royal chaplain. Great prelates, along with lay counts, often became Charles' *missi dominici*, or traveling envoys, who carried the emperor's commands to the far-flung reaches of the empire, and who saw that they were carried out. Alcuin, bred in the cathedral school of York, became Charlemagne's mentor in the establishment of the famous palace schools. Here the emperor's sons, as well as those of the nobility, were taught how to read and given hitherto unwonted appreciation of learning. Both cathedral and monastic schools sprang up. The era of Charles and his pious son Louis saw a renaissance of cultural scholarship. Though not highly original, it preserved the learning of the past by the precise monkish handwriting that multiplied precious manuscripts in neat Caroline miniscule (a uniform type of handwriting to which our Roman variety is closely related). Besides the English Alcuin, the Visigoth Theodulf, the East Frank Eginhard, the Lombard Paul the Deacon, and the Irishman John Erigena, all churchmen from various corners of the empire had their contributions to make to this intellectual revival. This variety of scholarship was a tribute to the breadth of Carolingian imperial vision.

Charlemagne thought of himself as the leader of the Christian people, and his empire was St. Augustine's famed city of God. Because the Church was a part of that city, it fell under his charge. Though he recognized the spiritual authority of the pope, the pope remained the emperor's subject. While Charles *defended* the city of God against the heathen, it was the pope's duty to *pray* to the God of victories.

Promise Unfulfilled

In 792 and in 794, Charlemagne summoned 2 synods to condemn the Adoptionist heretics who came out of Spain denying Christ's divinity. Though a defender of the faith, Charles was not beyond challenging the Church's correct teaching concerning the proper use of images and pictures in religious worship. In 794, at the synod of Frankfort, the emperor condemned their use, though approved by the ecumenical Council of Nicaea (787), and he unsuccessfully demanded that the pope support his decision. Despite the objections of the pope, the Franks insisted on adding the word *filioque* to the Nicene Creed and thus stirred up a controversy with the Eastern Church which strongly objected to anyone tampering with a creed of faith.

If the Carolingian kings and emperors were characterized by their generosity to the Church, they were never above taking back the lands of a monastery or a cathedral and bestowing them upon a knight in order to assure his loyalty. Nevertheless, when all was said and done, the Church flourished in their hands. Under Pepin the Short, St. Boniface carried out the reform of the Frankish Church by the establishment of bishoprics and metropolitan sees. He also brought the faith to Germany as a missionary. Under Charlemagne the Christian religion became the bond of unity in the new Western Empire. The emperor of the Christian people imposed his faith on his captive subjects in Northern and Central Europe. Resented or not, Christianity took root and defeated the more barbaric aspects of paganism. A strong succession of Western emperors might have guaranteed the maturing of Christianity that the Carolingian renaissance had promised. However, in 843, when Charlemagne's empire was divided among his 3 ambitious grandsons as their personal inheritance, the world of the West stood upon the threshold of civil war and cultural chaos. All the promise of the Carolingian revival was cut short as the West stepped back into barbarism.

Discussion Questions

1. How did the old Roman Empire, centered in Constantinople, lose its grip on western Europe?

2. Did the popes, as Roman citizens, betray the Roman Empire by calling on the Franks for protection?

3. Discuss the Church's role in forming the Holy Roman Empire of Charlemagne.

4. Discuss Charlemagne's attitude toward himself as religious leader of the People of God. What effect has this attitude had on subsequent secular rulers?

5. Why was the Roman Catholic Church the "blood" of Charlemagne's empire?

Chapter 6
The First Reformation

—————————— Some of Christ's Fragile Fellowship ——————

Pope John XII (d. 964) — made the papacy a family affair.
Henry III (972-1024) — the Saxon emperor who shaped up the papacy.
Odo of Cluny (c. 879-942) — the monk who saved the Church by silence.
John of Gorze (d.c. 975) — busy monk who shouted for change.
Gregory VII (c. 1021-1085) — the Roman pope who slapped down a Saxon emperor.

Amid all its splendors, the fundamental weakness of the Carolingian Empire was its lack of any idea of the state. The emperor was really a tribal leader and what he had, he divided among his sons, as if his realm were his own private property. No law of succession governed the passing of political power upon the emperor's death. To carve up the empire and battle over the pieces was the unhappy solution of this ideological inadequacy. By 888, after a series of civil wars that pitted brother against brother and bishop against bishop, the empire of Charlemagne was no more. Odo, count of Paris, became the king of Francia, while Berengarius of Friuli and Guy of Spoleto vied with each other to dominate Italy. Later, in the 10th century, the Holy Roman Empire revived under the Saxon kings and a semblance of order and culture was restored, but the old days of Charlemagne never returned.

Besides the civil wars fought over bits of Charlemagne's empire, the Vikings came to disrupt the peace of Christendom. As early as the first decade of the 9th century, the great Charles himself had had to fight these Scandinavian brigands on the north coast of France. These Northmen left the cold inhospitality of Denmark or Norway to see what they could seize by their swords and their wits from the monasteries and manors that sat undefended along the English and Irish coast. Sailing south to

France, the Vikings raided its channel shore as far south as the Loire, there moving upstream to devastate its valley towns. Granted land around Rouen, the Vikings became Normans and settled down to work the land. Though their raiding days were over by the beginning of the 10th century, the descendants of these sea rovers seized the throne of England at the battle of Hastings in 1066.

While the booty-hungry Vikings, in their dragon-prowed long ships, burned or carried off the civilization of England, Ireland, and Northern France, Hungarian barbarians pierced the empire's Eastern frontier. Laying waste to central Germany, the Hungarians continued to menace Christendom until the middle of the

10th century, when they suffered a decisive trouncing at Lechfeld (Augsburg).

Christian Loss of Nerve

Though probably not planned, the barbarians from the North and East struck at the very moment when the empire, torn by civil strife, could least afford them. The various princes of the divided empire were busily fighting each other for survival, so there was little aid that they could send to relieve the empire's hard-pressed frontiers. Local nobles, with large lands and a fortified manor house, or walled monasteries with numerous retainers defended the helpless peasants of the area. More and more, these people came to look to the large local landowner, whether he was layman or monk, as the source of law and order in the community. The word of the local count or abbot (and sometimes he was both) became law, for he alone had the power to enforce it. This cut the heart out of any central imperial authority. Western Europe became a patchwork quilt of local authorities vying for power, and the system called feudalism was born.

Religious life could hardly hope to come out of this upheaval unscathed. Even in the high tide of Charlemagne, monastic discipline had slipped. For certain lay lords were endowed by the emperor with monasteries as a source of income. There they lived with their wives and families. Supporting them was not only a drain upon monastic finances; the fighting, hawking, dancing, and sometimes wenching of their daily lives was not calculated to have a healthy effect upon monastic discipline.

During the civil wars of the 9th century, monasteries and cathedrals often found themselves the centers of opposition and were frequently attacked and pillaged. What the Franks spared, the Vikings, Hungarians, or Mohammedan Saracens of the Mediterranean seized. Monks, living on the sea or on any navigable river, were forced to flee or be hacked to pieces by pagan Vikings. Uprooted from the tranquillity of their monasteries, often without enough to eat, it was little wonder that the religious life of the monks suffered.

Priestly Politicians

The Carolingian emperors depended upon churchmen for the smooth running of the empire. In general, their choice of bishops, men often well-trained in the imperial chapel schools, was good. But, as the empire crumbled and was gradually divided up among the nobility, the quality of churchmen often left something to be desired. A duke might appoint his younger brother, or a cousin, to rule over an episcopal see within his duchy. Because the Church would own large tracts of land, the duke would need someone upon whom he could always depend. His concern was mainly to find fidelity to himself in his bishop, not necessarily sanctity. To insure that fidelity, the bishop would swear homage to his duke for the Church land entrusted to his care. He swore to counsel his duke when asked, and to come to the duke's aid with troops when needed. In return, the duke invested the bishop with the signs of his episcopal authority, his ring and crozier. Because the duke was usually a layman, this ceremony was known as lay investiture.

Though understandable when one considers the uncertainties of the times, the system of lay investiture was easily open to abuses. It seemed to give the temporal power authority over the spiritual. Putting the appointment of bishops into the hands of a powerful noble invited unworthy candidates to apply for the job. For being a bishop could be a profitable affair indeed. The incomes of some sees were considerable, and there were always enterprising scoundrels about who were willing to pay for the privilege of being a bishop. This particular racket was called simony, because it reminded people of Simon Magus attempting to bribe St. Peter into showing him how he worked his miracles. The simoniacal churchman usually lived as a lay lord, more at home in the saddle with sword in hand than in the sanctuary of his cathedral, mitered and croziered. He was no stranger to the enticements of wine and women, and his lust for money generally won for him the hatred of his flock.

The Priestly Proletariat

The spiritual condition of the parish priests of the 10th and 11th centuries was not happy. Most had been appointed to their parish by the wealthiest landowner of the district who had often built the church. It was this landowner who usually helped himself to the lion's share of the parish revenues, paying the curate as little as he had to. Without adequate religious or intellectual training, there was little to distinguish the parish priest from his peasant parishioners. To supplement his income, the priest not only worked a plot of ground but he often had a job, perhaps plying his trade as a cooper or a brewer. In most cases, he violated his vow of celibacy by living with a woman.

This scandal of a clergy married without benefit of clergy was commonplace, though it remained a stumbling block to the people and was constantly condemned by the Church. Some priests protested that on their small salaries they could never survive without the budgetary abilities of a woman in the house!

When the Papacy Became a Plaything

Though the 9th century could boast of a strong pope, such as Nicholas I, the years between 896 and 964 saw perhaps the worst representation of pontiffs that the Church has ever had to suffer. The Carolingian emperors may have interfered in ecclesiastical affairs, but, once their heavy, protecting hand was gone, the papacy became a plaything of the Roman aristocracy. The family of Theophylact, controlling the impregnable Castel Sant' Angelo, decisively also controlled the papal court from the end of the 9th century to the middle of the 10th. Though most of the popes of this period were not so vile as they have been painted, for the most part, they were do-nothings, prisoners of the Roman nobility. Pope John XII (955-964), a prince of the house of Theophylact, however, was very probably totally debauched and completely unworthy of his high office.

In 964, Otto the Great, the first Holy Roman Emperor of the German Nation, intervened in papal affairs and deposed John XII. He named several popes and set the trend for imperial intervention. The popes nominated by the German emperors were of high quality, especially Pope Sylvester II (999-1003). However, the power of the Roman aristocracy was not dead, and one or the other mighty family was able to impose one of its own creatures upon the papal throne. Benedict IX, an enterprising reincarnation of John XII, planned to marry his cousin, perhaps plotting to make the papal tiara hereditary. Once again, a German emperor, Henry III, came to the rescue by replacing the ambitious Benedict with a competent man of his own.

Resurrection from the Rubble

In the beginning of the 10th century, when the last monasteries had been raided and the lure of good land in Normandy or Danelaw, in England, called them from their dragon ships, the Vikings settled down to farming. In that same hour, monks all over Europe came from the charred ruins of their monasteries and attempted to start over again. In England, St.

59

Dunstan of Canterbury restored the discipline of his monastery of Glastonbury, and so great was his fame that his reforming spirit was felt as far south as Austria. In 910, Berno, the abbot of Baume, acting with the aid of William, the duke of Aquitaine, laid the foundations of the new monastery of Cluny in Burgundy. Cluny was to follow the rule of St. Benedict, but the choir monks were to do no manual labor. Silence was strictly guarded, broken only by the chanting of the *Opus Dei*, the liturgical office. The beauty of this public prayer was to be the sole work of the monks of Cluny. To keep monastic discipline at white heat, William of Aquitaine bestowed all the monastic lands upon the Holy See. Cluny was to have no lay patron who might disturb the order of the house and drain off its revenues. The monks had the right to elect their own abbot, and the abbot owed responsibility to the pope alone. So effective was this reform of Cluny that soon princes and bishops invited the monastery to found daughter houses in their territories. By the year 1100, Cluny could count 1,450 foundations spread over Western Europe, all following the same rule and linked by close bonds to the same mother house.

In Lombardy, St. Romuald founded the Camaldolese Order, whose members, seeking closer union with God, lived in separate cells like hermits, meeting together only for their meager meals. Their monastery of Fonte Avellana enjoyed a great renown for sanctity in the 11th century, and St. Romuald became a forerunner of St. Bruno, who founded the Carthusians, an order so fervent that it has never been in need of reform.

Stricter, but much more loosely knit, were the reformed monasteries of Lorraine and Southern Germany which followed the lead of Jean de Vandieres and his monks of Gorze. Emphasizing hard work, long fasts, and vigils, the spirit of Jean of Gorze restored a rigid discipline to monastic houses in Toul, Metz, Liège, Mainz, Cologne, and Salzburg.

The monastic reform of the 10th and 11th centuries, modest as it was, spread beyond the walls of its cloisters. The fiery sermons of these monks, coupled with their austere example, influenced the lives of the diocesan clergy to a greater or lesser extent. Many monks left their monasteries to become bishops where they could force their dioceses to accept reform. The Cluniac practice of direct dependence upon the Holy See probably enhanced the authority of the popes and tended to make each daughter house of Cluny a finger of the Holy See in England, France, and Germany. The carrying out of monastic reform on a private scale set the stage for the second act in the cleansing of the Church, official reform, this time stemming from the papacy itself.

Gregory VII Shapes Up the Church

As popes of high caliber once again sat upon the papal throne, they realized the need for universal reform in the Church. Several popes of the 11th century had been monks in monasteries that had been touched by the burning words of Jean of Gorze or the fierce fasts and scourgings of Peter Damien, monk of Fonte Avellana and, finally, cardinal of Ostia. Others came from Cluny or one of her daughter houses. They realized that, if the Church was racked with impurity and worldliness, it was because laymen in high places had the power to appoint anyone they wished to important dioceses or monasteries. Taking this power from lay hands and restoring it to the Church would go a long way toward cleaning up impure priests and monks who often had won their office by sale to the highest bidder.

In order to make sure that worthy men became bishops and abbots, Pope Gregory VII first of all appealed to the German emperor, Henry IV, the king of France, Philip I, and the Norman conqueror of England, William of Falaise, to cooperate with the spiritual needs of the Church in making their ecclesiastical appointments. Philip of France ignored the pope's appeal. Many German bishops grumbled against Gregory's interference in their Church. Though William the Conqueror favored the pope's ideas on reform, one of his bishops, John of Avranches, was stoned by his clergy when he warned them to get rid of their concubines.

Since this attempt at reform on a local level was less than successful, Pope Gregory decided to impose it upon the entire Church. At the Roman Synod of 1074, he revived all the decrees that forbade any layman, whether emperor, king, or noble, from bestowing spiritual power upon priests. He also put teeth into the laws defending clerical celibacy. He let it be known that he would no longer tolerate bishops like Rombaldo of Fiesoli who was "surrounded by a swarm of women," or Denis of Piacenza "who knew more about judging feminine beauty than he did about judging fit men to be clerics."

61

The Showdown at Canossa

Instead of relying upon the local bishop to enforce his law, Pope Gregory sent his own trusted legates into each country armed with bulls of excommunication for anyone who resisted them. And there were those who resisted, not the least of whom was the German emperor, Henry IV. Because he could not count upon the loyalty of his ambitious nobles, he depended upon bishops, whom he could make or break, to enforce his power in the far-flung cities of the German empire. Henry was bound to resist any papal decree that would deprive him of the power of naming bishops, the mainstay of his empire. Gregory VII excommunicated the resisting emperor in 1076, and then released his subjects from their allegiance to him, for in the pope's eyes Henry was nothing but a heretic and no Christian was bound to obey him. This was the opening gun in the 200-year war that was to set pope against emperor. The nobles of the empire, jealous of Henry's overbearing attitude, were only too glad to side with the pope and find another emperor whom they could more easily control. To save his empire from disintegration, in 1077 Henry IV knelt in the January snows of Canossa, in Italy, until Gregory VII lifted the ban of excommunication that made him an outcast of Christendom.

But his humiliation taught him nothing, and it was not long before he was banned from the Church again. The battle over bishops between popes and emperors lasted until the unsatisfactory Concordat of Worms in 1122.

By this agreement, a man appointed or elected to a bishopric would receive the symbols of his temporal authority from his duke, king, or emperor and swear fidelity for the civil power lodged in episcopal lands. Only after that would the Church consecrate him bishop and present him with the symbols of his spiritual authority, his episcopal ring, and crosier. Many a loophole appeared in this overly subtle procedure, and the battle over lay investiture continued into the 19th century. Strangely enough, what the Church could not obtain from Catholic states, she often willingly received from countries either hostile or indifferent to her. In the democratic states of the 19th and 20th centuries, the principle of total separation, where honestly adhered to, has scrupulously left the appointment of bishops in ecclesiastical hands.

The Popes Run the Church

The struggle over reform in the 10th and 11th centuries strengthened the Church internally. Gregory VII's campaign against Henry IV weakened the authority of the German emperors and set the stage for a continuing conflict that would destroy the political power of the empire and papacy as well. For all that, it loosened the strangle hold that the emperors had upon the Church. By imposing much needed reforms through papal legates, oftentimes brusquely overruling or deposing uncooperative bishops or metropolitans, the papacy left no doubt about its total authority in the running of the Church. This centralization in papal power grew. In the 12th and 13th centuries, more and more episcopal appointments stemmed from Rome rather than from the will of kings or from elections. Rome also more closely supervised the Catholic schools throughout Europe. The number of appeals from local ecclesiastical courts to the Holy See increased, and the papacy reserved for herself the right to call holy Catholics "saints." Some theorists, who had acted as public relations men for Pope Gregory VII, began to feel that the Church was, and always had been, superior to the state because Christ, they claimed, had placed all authority in her hands. As the Middle Ages pass along, this theory will grow both as a support and as an embarrassment to popes battling for life with ambitious German emperors and French kings.

Gregory VII may not have settled the lay investiture question, but he firmly established the claim of the papacy to rule the whole Church. The strength of the papacy's grip upon the Church and the way Christians reacted to it will form the subject of most of the ensuing chapters.

Discussion Questions

1. What effect did civil wars and the barbarian invasion of the Vikings and the Hungarians have upon the political unity of Western Europe?
2. How did the chaos of the 9th and 10th centuries affect Christ's fragile fellowship?
3. What was feudalism?
4. How did feudalism disturb the Church?

5. Discuss the 11th century as the era of the Church's first Reformation. Compare it with the 16th century second Reformation of the Church.

Chapter 7
Political Power Falls to the Popes

Ten seventy-one was a very bad year for the Byzantine Empire (so called because the ancient name for Constantinople was Byzantium).

In the West, Bari, the last Byzantine stronghold on the Italian Peninsula, fell to the Normans. Originally coming into the area as pilgrims, the Normans accepted the invitation of local Lombard dukes to return in force and help them rid the countryside of Greeks. They returned and, properly land hungry, drove out the Byzantines, keeping the real estate for themselves. The second Norman conquest within 5 years (the first being England in 1066) came off brilliantly with the fall of Bari. Within a mere 20 years, the South of Italy and Sicily would be largely in Norman hands.

In August 1071, on the eastern frontier, the Seljuk Turks defeated the Byzantines (some Greeks claimed it was due to the treachery of a group of Frankish mercenaries in Byzantine employ), poured into Asia Minor, and eventually occupied the Holy Land. Fanatically Mohammedan, they harassed Christian pilgrimages to the holy places in and around Jerusalem, and they threatened the very survival of the Byzantine Empire.

Willy-nilly, the year of Constantinople's discontent marks the beginning of the rise of the papacy to political preeminence in Christendom.

Political Rivalry Cloaked in Religion

As we have seen, the barbarian invasions and the creation of Charlemagne's new Roman Empire of the West strained relations between the East and West almost to the breaking point. Though differences in religious usages in the Eastern and Western Catholic Churches (Greek vs. Latin in liturgical languages, leavened vs. unleavened bread in the Eucharist, bearded vs. unbearded clergymen, married vs. unmarried priests) paint a picture of theological controversy, the real problem was political ambition aroused and denied. How concerned was Charlemagne with theological orthodoxy when he defied the orthodox canons of the ecumenical Council of Nicaea (787) concerning the veneration due to sacred images? His real reason may well have been to lessen the prestige of the Eastern Roman Empire that stood in opposition to his own political dreams of imperial domination. The Frankish addition of the word *filioque* to the Nicene Creed, when analyzed closely, represents no real *religious* parting of the ways between East and West. Most Eastern theologians had no fight with the theological nuance the addition of the Latin word made clear. They properly, and somewhat snobbishly, resented barbarian Franks tampering with a creed of an ecumenical council. Specious religious differences cloaked very real social and political rivalries and created a crusading atmosphere that would canonize hostile military activities and eventually destroy the Byzantine Empire in the name of religion.

Charlemagne's Western Roman Empire possessed a fluid eastern frontier that bordered upon the western stretches of the Byzantine Empire. Into the present-day country of Yugoslavia and Northern Greece poured pagan Slavic barbarians, mainly Bulgars, who admired the Roman Empire and sought a parcel of its land. Byzantium (Constantinople) envisioned a commonwealth of Eastern nations circling in her enlightened orbit, making the world safe for civilization. When the Byzantine emperors looked to their northwestern frontier, they saw Franks of the Latin Church ready, willing, and often able to thwart their imperial vision. In the competition for Slavic souls, Frankish-Latin missionaries, with allegiance to Rome and the Roman Empire of the West, vied with Greek missionaries whose loyalties were sworn to Byzantium. When pagan Slavs became Latin Catholics along the southeastern frontiers of present-day Austria, Byzantium noted, with growing rancor, that they also became members of the Frankish-Latin Empire and increased its population and power. The so-called Photian schism of 861 and afterward is an example of how politics worked to the disservice of religious unity.

The Fight over Photius

In 858 when the Byzantine emperor, Michael III, appointed his scholarly and saintly imperial secretary, Photius, to be patriarch of the Church of Constantinople, it was under more

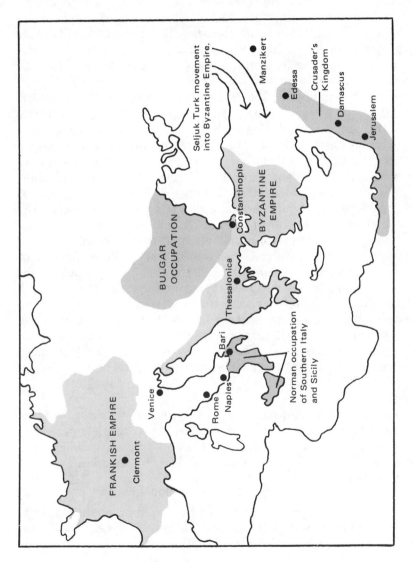

than highly suspicious circumstances. The emperor had arbitrarily deposed his predecessor, St. Ignatius, on charges amounting to high treason. When Pope Nicholas I learned of Photius' appointment, he demanded that the case of Ignatius be reexamined by legates representing the pope in Constantinople. Reluctantly, but as a sign of Byzantine respect for the pope's religious authority, Michael III consented. The papal legates, convinced that Ignatius had suffered no injustice at the emperor's hands, returned to Pope Nicholas and counseled his acceptance of Photius as patriarch. Pope Nicholas, who wanted direct control of the Greek Church of Thessalonica (in Greece), which he intended to rule with a vicar, made his acceptance of Photius depend upon the Byzantine emperor's consent to his plans. The emperor, fearing that Roman rule of the Thessalonian Church would inevitably weaken Byzantine political power in Greece, refused to give in to the pope. Religious controversy followed with Photius pot-shotting at all the differences in religious usage between East and West. The theological fireworks were mainly for the benefit of the pagan Bulgars who had moved into Northern Greece and Dalmatia (Yugoslavia). Their king, Boris, was seeking which brand of Catholicism, Eastern or Western, he and his people should choose, for he was a convinced believer in the amenities of Roman civilization, and he was also convinced (more so than many of his people) that to be a Roman you had to be a Catholic. To convince the Bulgars of the orthodoxy of the Byzantines, Photius attacked the Frankish addition of the *filioque* to the Nicene Creed, bemoaned the fact that Frankish "heretical" missionaries were trying to convert the Bulgars, and promptly excommunicated the so-called heretic pope, Nicholas. The schism between East and West that ensued was eventually repaired in the years 879-80 when the Holy See recognized Photius as patriarch, but only after King Boris and his Bulgars became Greek Catholics under bishops with loyalties to Constantinople.

Though the Photian crisis passed, it left festering wounds. And Photius himself, a great and prolific writer, left behind an arsenal of literary ammunition that could be convincingly used as anti-Roman propaganda, should a future need arise.

The Papacy Plays International Politics

As long as the papacy remained a plaything of the powerful Roman families, its international prestige remained at low ebb. But when the Saxon emperors put churchmen of quality upon the papal throne — men imbued with the reforming spirit of Cluny and Gorze — sooner or later they were bound to tangle with the snobbish spirit of Byzantine sophistication and assumed superiority over Western "Franks" (a catch-all word of contempt applied to all Westerners, whatever their ethnic origins, and meaning loutish, ruthless barbarians).

In 1027 a group of Norman adventurers began the first Norman conquest when they took the fortress of Aversa near Naples. The land of Southern Italy belonged to the Byzantines and Lombards, and the papacy became their ally in attempting to resist the inroads of these latter-day Vikings.

The patriarch of the Church of Constantinople, Michael Cerularius, was perhaps the most powerful churchman to ever occupy the Byzantine See. Detesting the Latin "Franks" and fully convinced that the Church had authority over the state, Michael tried to scotch, in every way, the anti-Norman alliance of Pope Leo IX and the Byzantine emperor, Constantine IX. He accused the emperor's deputy in Italy, a Lombard named Argyrus, of heresy. Byzantine churchmen, priests and monks, churned out religious diatribes condemning Latin practices and embittered the populace of Constantinople against the Roman Church. All of this was embarrassing to the Byzantine emperor who badly needed an Italian ally against the land-hungry Normans.

Unfortunately for the Byzantine-papal alliance, the Normans defeated the pope's army at the battle of Civitate (1053) and took Leo IX prisoner. Pope Leo, trying to cope with the ambitious Byzantine patriarch, sent his legate, Cardinal Humbert of Moyenmoutier, to Constantinople to deal with Michael Cerularius. Humbert, afire with an uncompromising spirit of reform and fanatically devoted to the papacy, suffered upstarts badly, even if they were patriarchs of Constantinople. When Leo died, Michael struck at the late pope's legate by challenging his authority. In return, Humbert excommunicated Patriarch Michael during the liturgy in his own cathedral. The emperor, who sympathized with the papacy but who also knew that his people were with Michael, reluctantly acquiesced. This melee of diplomacy by excommunication took place in July 1054. Though the year marked no final break between the Church of the East and West, it clearly showed that the Byzantine people had little love for the Roman Church of the "Franks" and willingly challenged its role as the religious leader of Christendom.

The Popes Lead the First "Frankish" Expeditionary Force

An indication that the schism of 1054 was far from final came in 1071 when Manzikert fell to the Turks. The Byzantine emperor sent a call for help to Pope Gregory VII. He desired a small expeditionary force from the West to defend the beleaguered Byzantine Empire. Gregory had his hands full with the German emperor, Henry IV, and, though he favored such a crusade, he was in no position to organize one. Appeals from the East for aid in arms fell on deaf ears until Pope Urban II took up the cry for a crusade at the Synod of Clermont in 1095. When he called for volunteers to take the cross and rescue the holy places from the Moslem Turks, his enthusiastic listeners cried, "God wills it," and the first crusade was born.

By this time, the Normans occupied Southern Italy (and England) with the papal blessing, and younger sons of Norman families were looking for new worlds to conquer. It would be unfair to dismiss religious ideals as a motivating force in the first crusade, but it would also be naïve to think that the lust for new land moved no Norman to take the cross. It is quite possible that Pope Urban also recognized an opportunity to keep the peace in Western Europe by diverting landless and restless fighting men to the Middle East. Whatever motivated this "Frankish" expeditionary force, it arrived at the gates of Constantinople, upward of 50,000 strong and under the leadership of Bishop Adhemar, papal legate, in 1097.

The emperor, Alexius Comnenus, was shocked. He had hoped for a few thousand fighting men to reinforce his dwindling troops. But here was a horde of "Franks," many of whom had been his recent enemies in the Norman conquest of Southern Italy (Bohemund, Tancred), and he seriously wondered if his far-from-pious rescuers might not be more dangerous to his empire than his Moslem enemies. Faced with no alternatives, the emperor permitted his "Frankish" allies to invade the Holy Land. In the early summer of 1099, the crusaders took Jerusalem, massacred the Jewish and Moslem populace, and set up the Kingdom of Jerusalem, the third Norman conquest. The Kingdom of Jerusalem, a transplantation of Norman feudalism into the Middle East, survived until 1187 when Saladin, uniting all Moslem forces, drove the crusaders from the Holy City.

The Crusades Crush Constantinople

Prior to the fall of Jerusalem, the Turks had taken Edessa

(1044) from the crusaders. This prompted the papacy to call for a second crusade, this one recruited by a great saint, Bernard of Clairvaux. Louis VII of France and Conrad III of the Holy Roman Empire allied themselves with Baldwin III of Jerusalem and set out to conquer Damascus. Cut to pieces by quarreling and Moslem ambushes, this crusade suffered heavy casualties and collapsed, accomplishing nothing but the creation of an "anti-Vietnam" attitude toward crusading.

But the papacy was not to be denied its role as world religious leader. Pope Clement III, after Jerusalem's fall, appealed to Frederick Barbarossa of Germany, Philip II of France, and Richard the Lionhearted of England to wrest the holy places from Turkish hands. Happily for papal interests in the Italian Peninsula, the ambitious German emperor, Frederick, who had his eye on Italian real estate, drowned in Cilicia. Richard and Philip quarreled constantly, and the most the third crusade accomplished was a treaty with the Turks guaranteeing the safety of Christian pilgrims in the Holy Land (1192).

In 1199 Pope Innocent III called Christendom to a fourth crusade to liberate the Holy Land. Duped by the merchants of Venice, this crusade, instead of attacking Moslems, stormed the city of Constantinople in behalf of Venetian commercial interests and temporarily destroyed the Byzantine Empire. Though Pope Innocent III had disassociated himself from this Venetian enterprise, the Latin Empire of Constantinople came into existence in 1204. The Latin liturgy and Latin practices were imposed upon unwilling Greek Catholics until 1261 when the Byzantines recaptured Constantinople. If any year marks a permanent schism between the Church of the East and West, it is 1204. Though attempts at reunion were made until 1453, when the city fell to the Turks, no unity was practically possible. The Greeks, so embittered and humiliated by their "Frankish" conquerors, came to prefer the star and crescent of the Turks to the papal tiara.

The Catholic Church As Papal State

The crusading adventure, though a failure, established the Roman Catholic Church as a world religious leader. Gaining strength through the first reformation of the 10th and 11th centuries, it cleaned its own house under the vital leadership of the Holy See. But this reforming vitality poured over the frontiers of religion. The Roman Catholic Church became a political power to be conjured with in the growing national monarchies of Western Europe. And the Papal States became a monarchy like other monarchies, this one lodged midway down the Italian Peninsula. By the year 1204, due to his own abilities and the lack of competition, Pope Innocent III was doubtlessly the most powerful sovereign of the Western world. The papacy, actually involved in military adventures to enforce the will of the popes upon the Middle East and Constantinople, was far from reluctant to defend its Italian territory with indulgences, money, and blood from German emperors hungry for a place in the warm Roman sun. In the next 100 years, the successors of Innocent III would make the Italian Peninsula a wilderness of blood and carnage as they defended the Papal States' political interests against the encroachments of the Holy Roman Empire. As the image of the *Beautiful Savior* (one of the crusaders' favorite hymns) faded, the popes more and more resembled a mighty God going forth to war, and they antagonized their people who were more devoted to the Prince of Peace.

Discussion Questions

1. What were the political roots for the rivalry between the Catholic Church of the East and of the West?
2. Had you been alive at the time of the Photian crisis, which side would you have taken?
3. How did the first Reformation create the Roman Catholic Church as an international political power?
4. Compare the theological differences between the Roman Catholic Church and the Greek Orthodox Church with their political and sociological differences.
5. Discuss how the thrust of history made a king out of the vicar of Christ.

Chapter 8
Birth of a Papal Nation

———————— Some of Christ's Fragile Fellowship ————————

Ivo of Chartres (c. 1050-1116) — the great feudal compromiser.
Roger II Guiscard (1093-1154) — the other Norman conqueror.
Norbert of Premontré (c. 1080-1134) — the canon who thundered for change.
Albert the Great (c. 1200-1280) — theologian, scientist, evolutionist.
Roger Bacon (c. 1214-1292) — pioneer of experimental science.
Thomas Aquinas (c. 1225-1274) — the daring "angelic Doctor" who "baptized" Aristotle.

If it was association with the Frankish Empire and the organization and leadership of crusades against the Turks that made the papacy an international power, it was conflict with the German emperors over lay investiture that effectively brought into being a national entity in the Italian Peninsula called the Papal States. A determined refusal to allow German emperors to put their creatures into episcopal sees invited military reprisals upon the Patrimony of Peter, reprisals designed to force the popes into the acceptance of lay investiture.

To defend the geography of the Papal States and the principle of independence concerning episcopal appointees, the popes negotiated military alliances with the growing Western kingdoms of England, France, Norman Italy, and the independent city-states of Lombardy and Venice. To further discourage imperial aggression, the papacy plotted with rebel German princes who resented a strong emperor and centralized authority. Such disaffected princes kept the German Empire in the turmoil of civil war. If their rebellious attitude toward imperial authority guaranteed the survival of the Papal States as a political entity, it was disastrous to the ambitions of the German emperors who might have granted a badly needed political stability to Central Europe. In the long run, it undermined the peace and stability of the Italian Peninsula, torn by war, civil strife, and economic chaos. Gradually, many people of Europe began to identify Roman Catholicism with the political Papal States.

More and more, papal ecclesiastics began to endow the popes with growing political power to enhance their position in the struggle against the emperors. By the end of the 13th century, Pope Boniface VIII could practically claim that all authority, spiritual and political, was given to the papacy by Christ. By and large, national rulers did not take kindly to a theory that made them vassals of the popes. Resentments grew to such a point that the kings of France and England took measures to insure that the Catholic Church within their respective domains would become subservient to the state. And they initiated propaganda campaigns against papal political policy that tended to make citizens of the realm look upon the papacy as simply another Italian and, often, rival state. To be patriotic often meant to be antipapal, though one might remain a fervent Catholic.

The Lay Investiture Compromise

Though Emperor Henry IV received papal absolution at Canossa in 1077, the princes of the German Empire deposed him and named Rudolf of Swabia as his successor. Henry, never a retiring type, refused his dismissal, organized an army, and

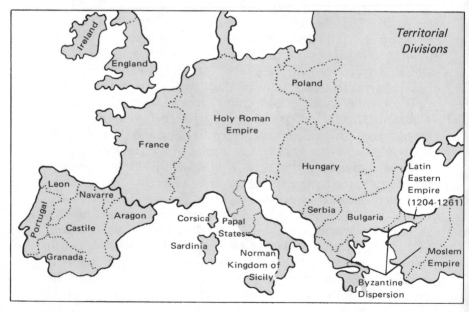

marched on Rome. After killing Rudolf of Swabia, the outlaw emperor seized the city. Pope Gregory VII, beseiged in the Castel Sant'Angelo, was rescued by his Norman allies who drove off Henry's troops and took Rome for themselves. No more gentle than the imperials, the Normans pillaged the city and withdrew to the South. Pope Gregory, no longer popular in Rome due to the depredations of his military allies, fled with the Normans to die an exile in Salerno in 1085.

It was left to Pope Urban II (1088-99), the first crusader, to settle with Henry. In close alliance with the freewheeling princes of the empire (Henry's wife and sons betrayed him) and the freedom-loving Northern Italian communes (like Milan, Pisa, Genoa, and the Republic of Venice), Urban forced Henry IV to abdicate in favor of his son, Henry V. Henry, *père*, died in exile in Liège in 1106, and was denied Christian burial.

But that was far from being the last act in the drama of who ran the Church. Henry V (1106-25), his father's son, continued to demand the right to invest "his" bishops with their sees. In 1110 the new emperor marched on Rome, seized Pope Paschal II (Urban's successor who was pope between 1099-1118), and forced him to concede the right of lay investiture. Once free, Paschal revoked his forced concession and the war began afresh. For nearly 12 years, Henry V battled rebellious princes of the empire who, for their own reasons, were the natural allies of the papacy. In 1119 a peacemaker pope, in the person of Calixtus II (1119-1124), appeared upon the scene. Calixtus, a member of the French nobility, was related to most of the crowned heads of Europe. The pope hit upon a compromise: Bishops and abbots were to be elected according to the laws of the Church; once elected, and before their consecration, the emperor could invest them with symbols of their civil authority, scepter and sword, and they, in their turn, would swear fidelity to the emperor for their civil power; then the Church would endow them with the symbols of their spiritual authority, their ring and episcopal staff, and consecrate them to their spiritual office for which they would do homage to the pope.

This concordat was signed with the emperor in 1122 and was proclaimed a law of the Church at Lateran Council I in 1123. Though it brought much-needed peace to a battle-weary empire, the compromise was not a totally happy solution. Theoretically, it neatly separated spiritual power from temporal, but, in practice, it conceded far too much authority to the emperors in

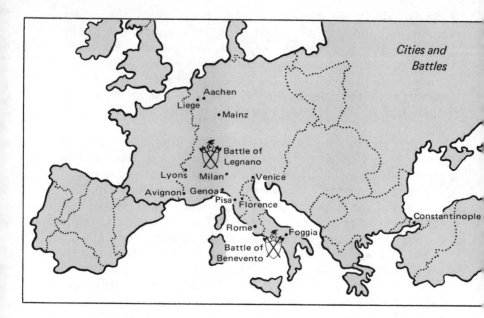

Cities and Battles

making ecclesiastical appointments. Practically speaking, it still remained difficult to distinguish a shepherd of the Church from a prince of the empire. As the concordat was valid only for the empire, possibly it was merely an agreement between Calixtus II and Henry V. Therefore, future conflict over lay investiture remained a real possibility and, indeed, has remained a bone of contention well into the 20th century.

The First Middle-class Revolt Against the Papacy

If the popes feared that the imperial embrace would crush them in a bear hug, they also had reason to fear the loss of imperial protection. Once again, in the year 1130, the papacy momentarily became the plaything of competing and powerful Roman families. Pope Innocent II (1130-1143), the protégé of the noble Roman Frangipani family, was elected to the papacy. A group of disaffected cardinals, however, elected a competitor pope, Peter Pierleoni. The Pierleonis were a rich merchant family in Rome. The election of Peter, who took the name Anacletus II, quite blatantly represented merchant middle-class resentment against the Roman nobility.

Innocent II, validly elected pope, had a strong champion of his cause in the eloquent "supersaint" of Europe, Bernard of Clairvaux (1090-1153). Bernard, a reforming Cistercian monk, hit the highways and byways of the continent in the cause of Innocent. He was able to convince Louis VI of France, Henry I of England, and the German emperor, Lothair III, of the justice of Innocent's claim to the papal tiara. Bernard also talked the cities of Genoa, Pisa, and Milan into accepting Innocent as pope.

In 1132-33 Lothair launched an attack upon Italy that failed to put Innocent permanently in the Vatican. Anacletus had allied his cause with the Normans of Sicily and Roger Guiscard, Sicily's uncrowned Norman king, drove Innocent out of Rome and turned the papacy over to Anacletus. In a back-scratching maneuver, Anacletus recognized the Norman adventurer Roger as king of Sicily.

In 1136 Pope Innocent II allied himself with the Emperor Lothair in an attempt to take Rome. But Roger II of Sicily repulsed every effort to unseat him. And (between 1137 and 1139), by fighting the pope, the emperor, the cities of Pisa, Genoa, Venice, and the Byzantine Empire, he actually established his sovereignty over Sicily and Southern Italy at the point of his sword.

Arnold of Brescia Leads the Merchants Against the Pope

In 1139 Roger made Innocent his prisoner. Since the anti-pope Anacletus had died in 1138, Roger recognized Innocent as the legitimate pope — in return for Innocent's acceptance of the Norman as king of Sicily. But the family fight was far from over.

With the papacy once again firmly ensconced in Rome, prosperity returned to the city. Church bureaucracy provided plenty of jobs, and pilgrims poured into the Vatican with coins for St. Peter's tomb and for Roman innkeepers. Merchants and members of the lesser nobility garnered the profit. And as they grew wealthy on the Church, proud memories of the ancient Roman Republic swelled their contempt for Rome's higher nobility, especially the cardinals of the curia and the pope himself. Commercial competition with neighboring cities degenerated into military campaigns. In 1143 Rome's rich merchants rose in revolt against the pope and set up a senate that excluded the Roman nobility. Jordan Pierleoni (the brother of Anacletus), independent of the pope, governed Rome as the "patrician" of the city. Violence in the streets marked this middle-class revolt, and Pope Lucius II, in 1145, probably died of wounds he received while leading an assault against the capitol.

Upon Lucius' death, a Cistercian monk who had once lived under St. Bernard at Clairvaux became pope. He took the name of Eugene III (1145-53). To complicate Eugene's precarious papacy, a forerunner of the 16th-century reformers appeared upon the turbulent Roman scene. He was an Augustinian monk (Martin Luther would be an Augustinian) named Arnold of Brescia. Arnold was a militant reformer who preached against Church wealth and Church political power. Condemned by St. Bernard and Lateran Council II (1139), Arnold came to Rome as a penitent in 1145. The middle-class merchant uprising was exactly to his liking, and, from penitent, Arnold emerged as tribune of the new Roman Republic. He denounced papal wealth and declared the republic free of papal politics. Both Eugene and Arnold called upon the new German emperor, Conrad III (1138-52), to defend their causes, but without avail. Conrad had his own civil wars in the empire. The Norman king of Sicily, Roger II, secured the papal throne for Eugene, but he also sustained the Roman Republic. Arnold remained a threat to the papacy until a strong German emperor, Frederick Barbarossa (1152-90), in alliance with Pope Hadrian IV (1154-59), captured Arnold and handed him over to the Roman prefect. The reformer met his God at the end of a hangman's noose in 1155.

The Hohenstaufen Grand Design of Empire

In Frederick Barbarossa, and the rest of his Hohenstaufen descendants, the popes faced adversaries every bit as imperious as Henry IV and far less pious than Arnold of Brescia. Lay investiture was no longer the issue. Empire was their thing. Beginning with Frederick I (Barbarossa), the Hohenstaufens endeavored to preserve a united German Empire. They wanted an empire that would finally dominate the Italian Peninsula and from there spill over the Mediterranean basin to create, once again, a single Roman Empire in the world. To frustrate this grand design were the Northern Italian city-states that valued their freedom, and the popes, who came to resolve that no strong northern power would ever also dominate the south of Italy and squeeze the Papal States out of existence. Quite naturally, the Normans in Southern Italy and the emperors in Constantinople were less than enthusiastic about Hohenstaufen ambitions.

When Frederick Barbarossa held Pope Hadrian IV's stirrup as

a sign of homage in 1155, it in no way indicated any inclination to be the pope's man. The gesture was worth imperial coronation at Hadrian's hands.

Frederick quelled civil disorder within the empire and extended its boundaries into Poland, Bohemia, and Hungary. But the red-bearded emperor was less successful in his Italian adventures. Though he tempted the Romans with dreams of a new Roman Empire, his seizure of Corsica and his suppression of the Lombard communes aroused the northern Italians into a willing alliance with the papacy. Between 1154-86 Frederick invaded Italy 6 times. On his fourth expedition (1166-68), the emperor took Rome away from Pope Alexander III (1159-81) and set up an antipope, Victor IV, in his place. But disease riddled his army and Frederick abandoned the Eternal City.

In 1176 Pope Alexander, allied with the Northern Italian city-states known as the Lombard League, cut Frederick's cavalry to pieces at the battle of Legnano and forced the frustrated emperor to negotiate the peace of Venice that recognized the communes' liberties and Alexander as pope. Lateran Council III (1179) confirmed the peace of Venice.

Reconciled with the Church, Frederick led the third crusade after Jerusalem's fall in 1187. His imperial frustrations drowned with him in the Saleph River in Cilicia in 1190.

Frederick's son, Henry VI, married Constance of Sicily, the heiress of the Norman Kingdom. Every bit his father's son, Henry's Norman marriage alliance threatened to squeeze the Papal States in a pincer's movement. Indeed, he planted German princes in the provinces north of the Papal States, and he was crowned king of Sicily in 1195. Only his premature death at the age of 30 (1197) saved the papacy from imperial domination.

The Popes Defend the Papal States

The early death of Henry VI snatched a strong man from Germany, and civil war once again scourged the empire. Claimants to the imperial throne had no time to devote to Italian conquest. And the Papal States played one off against the other to maintain territorial integrity.

But in Sicily was a sign of contradiction. Born in 1194 and bereft of both mother and father by 1198, Frederick II, son of Henry VI, became the ward of Pope Innocent III (1198-1216). Frederick was a true Hohenstaufen with an Italian accent. Brought up in the Norman court of Sicily, his outlook was far more Italian than German. Like his father before him, Frederick dreamed of a strong Italian state that would be the nucleus of a new Roman Empire. And Frederick, of all the German emperors, came closest to the stature of Charlemagne. He had the ability to carry it off successfully.

Because Innocent III recognized Frederick's unique potential for uniting Germany and Italy into one empire, he sought to put restraints upon the royal youth. Before he became emperor, the pope demanded homage to the Holy See. Once emperor, Frederick swore that he would go on a crusade, a diversionary tactic that the popes had found so useful in dealing with the young man's truculent grandfather, Frederick Barbarossa.

In 1209 Innocent III, aided by King Philip II of France, invited the 15-year-old Frederick to take the empire from Otto of Brunswick. Frederick, helped by Hohenstaufen followers, did just that.

Frederick II, crowned emperor in 1220, looked upon Germany as a service pool of men and resources. To assure himself of German peace, the new emperor granted many privileges of rule to the German princes and bishops and assured himself of their cooperation while he fleshed out his imperial dream in Italy.

When Pope Honorius III (1216-27) crowned him emperor in 1220, Frederick vowed to go on crusade. But uprisings in Sicily against Hohenstaufen rule made it impossible to keep his vow. In 1225 Frederick married Isabella, the heiress of the Frankish Kingdom of Jerusalem. Although the Mohammedans occupied the city, Frederick claimed the crown of the old crusader kingdom. In 1227, Frederick set out on crusade, but fever aboard his ships forced him to abort this attempt. Pope Gregory IX (1227-41), far from satisfied with Frederick's faltering efforts, excommunicated the emperor. Frederick, goaded by Gregory, once again took up the cross and successfully negotiated a treaty with the Turks, opening the city of Jerusalem to Christian pilgrims. Apparently, the excommunicated emperor's success infuriated Gregory IX; the pope invaded Sicily with papal troops, an invasion that Frederick returned to thwart.

The Popes Destroy Frederick's Grand Design

But now it was out in the open. The Papal States could not tolerate an empire that would dominate the Italian Peninsula. Pope Gregory returned to the old alliance with the Northern Italian communes. A propaganda campaign besmirching Frederick as a heretic and blasphemer, in fact, the anti-Christ, was unleashed with the greatest ferocity. And new battles in the name of religion ensued.

Pope Innocent IV (1243-54), not able to count upon the loyalty of the Romans, left the Papal States and lived in France. In 1245 he called the first Council of Lyons, where he excommunicated and deposed the emperor and preached a crusade to destroy him. In 1250, Frederick died, a broken man, near Foggia.

But the battle against the Hohenstaufens continued. In 1263 Pope Urban IV (1261-64), a Frenchman, invited Charles of Anjou, the brother of King St. Louis IX, to take over Southern Italy. At the battle of Benevento (1266), the French prince defeated and killed Manfred, Frederick's natural son. In this way, the French became involved in Italian politics with the help of the Papal States. But the people of Sicily, the nervous emperor of Constantinople, Michael VIII Paleologus (who saw in Charles a potential conqueror of the Mediterranean basin), and the expanding power of Aragon — all these resented this French domination. In 1282 the native Sicilians, perhaps secretly aided by the Aragonese, slaughtered French garrisons in Sicily and opened a 20-year war that finally conceded Sicily to the house of Aragon (1302).

If papal political policy succeeded in blocking the unification of the Italian Peninsula under one imperial authority, it also created the image of the Papal States as a political entity defending a national policy of survival through the use of troops and entangling foreign alliances. Devoid of the strength of imperial protection, papal policy could not stop the proliferation of powerful middle-class city-states to the north that fed upon each other through force of arms and mercantile competition. Both in the North and in the South, Catholic brother was turned against brother in the cause of papal or imperial ideals. Eventually the Papal States, torn with civil strife, became so unsafe that the papacy abandoned Rome and took up residence in Avignon in France (1309-78) just to survive. In destroying the empire, the political entity called the Papal States very nearly became its own undertaker.

Discussion Questions

1. How did the first Reformation of the 11th century bring the papacy into conflict with the Holy Roman Empire?

2. Trace the evolution of Peter's office in the Catholic Church from vicar of Christ to the ruler of a national state.

3. Can the Church guide or even coerce the consciences of secular rulers?

4. How does Pope Innocent II's conflict with the middle-class Pierleoni family presage future difficulties with a growing trend toward democracy?

5. Did ruling the Papal States distract the popes as leaders of Christ's Church?

Chapter 9
The Restless Marriage
of Church and State

————————Some of Christ's Fragile Fellowship————————

El Cid (c. 1040-1099) — Iberian crusader and cosmopolitan.

Stigand of Canterbury (d. 1072) — Saxon saint or scoundrel?

Lanfranc of Bec (c. 1005-1089) — gave the English Norman Church a continental look.

Gilbert Foliot (d. 1188) — the bishop who was baffled by Becket.

Blanche of Castile (1188-1252) — Christian mother and incontestable queen.

Giotto di Bondone (c. 1267-1336) — human beings have feelings.

As in the Holy Roman Empire, revived by the Saxons, local counts and dukes were willing to theoretically acknowledge the overlordship of an emperor, so also did the feudal strongmen of France and England theoretically acknowledge the existence of national kings. But in practice, both in the empire and in the developing Western nations, sword-wielding local nobles resented and obstructed, in varying degrees, the real power of growing monarchy. Local princes got rich upon a monopoly of power over a limited parcel of land and people. National authority might reach into their bailiwicks; by force of national arms it might restrain their profitable raiding expeditions upon a neighbor's castle and villages. This enforcement of national law and order sounded the death knell to self-aggrandizement. But the empire always had in huge supply rebel princes to harass and curtail imperial authority, keeping the domain in a perpetual state of war.

In medieval Europe an emperor or a king had to work at his job to make his authority felt. The emperors of the Holy Roman Empire failed. It took the kings of France some 800 years to create a national state. In England, where monarchy survives to this day, it owes its survival to an evolving democratic process that ran from the 13th to the 20th century. And destiny has yet to divine the final authority of the Spanish state.

Two natural allies of kingly authority in the West were the men of commerce who settled in cities and the clergy of the Roman Catholic Church.

Merchants favored hardy kingly government that would sweep the roads and riverways of robber barons waiting in ambush to bushwhack commerce. A national government would standardize coinage and weights and measures; would establish national customs' fees that would enable commerce to flow widely and smoothly free of fiscal harassment from castle to castle; would encourage the development of cities with charters of liberties given to their businessmen inhabitants in exchange for monetary subsidies.

Churchmen favored national authority because a strong king could keep the peace within the realm. And peace favored religion.

Bishops Belonged to the System

Yet, the city man's stance toward kingly authority was far less ambiguous than the cleric's. Emperors and kings of the Western world considered themselves to be the leaders of the People of God, just as Charlemagne had. The creation of the nation called the Papal States in the center of the Italian boot put popes at loggerheads with Charlemagne's pious imperial ideal. And this national papal consciousness was largely born of the reforming ideals of the 10th and the 11th centuries. By forcefully resisting imperial or kingly interference in the running of the Catholic Church, the reforming popes conceived the Church as a society, perfect in itself, protected by ancient liberties and privileges (eventually codified into a canon of law) that put it theoretically beyond the pale of kingly authority. Where monarchs attempted to curtail these liberties in the interests of a smoothly running state, it became, at least theoretically, the duty of churchmen to resist. The papal struggle against the emperors exemplified the stance.

On the other hand, the Church was very much of the Western medieval world. Bishops and abbots of the West held extensive lands of the kings' or emperors' domains to support the Church. For these lands they contracted obligations of loyalty toward their overlords as any other lay vassals. Being a bishop was an important job often reserved to brothers and cousins of kings. These churchmen, and others less nobly endowed, no matter how dedicated they were to Christ, were also members of the system with important roles to play in aiding their king with advice, monetary subsidies, and armed men for the defense of the realm. Little wonder high Church leaders could suffer the trauma of divided loyalties. A Church that regarded itself as an independent society, yet dependent on large landholdings (sources of power and wealth for which the piper had to be paid) to maintain its existence, was continually bound to collide with national monarchs whose power also almost totally depended upon real estate.

The English Marriage of Church and State

The reforming popes of the 11th century treated William the Conqueror (1027-87) with kid gloves. He was a firm sovereign who ran a clean Church in his realm of England and his holdings in France.

But conflict was bound to come with the reformed Church. King William II (1059-1100) considered selling bishoprics a profitable business and ran afoul his archbishop, St. Anselm,

and the papacy. William's brother and successor, Henry I, insisted upon an oath of fealty from every bishop and abbot in the realm because with their Church offices went extensive landholdings that made them as powerful as any lay nobleman. When Henry II (1133-1189) inherited the English crown in 1154, after nearly 20 years of civil war and chaos, he was

Henry II

determined to restore law and order to England. This he did by putting down a restless and rebellious nobility.

His fight with the Catholic Church in his realm was really a personality conflict between himself and his archbishop, St. Thomas of Canterbury (1118-1170). Determined to bring justice to England, he sought to punish clerics who committed civil crimes with the firm justice of civil courts. (Clerics were men who received a minor order in the Church, often for the purpose of gaining a formal education, so that they could be clerks in the king's or some nobleman's court. They were subject to Church law, but often followed no religious calling. Every priest was a cleric, but not every cleric was a priest.

About one-sixth of England's population was clerical.) St. Thomas Becket, the archbishop of Canterbury, and Henry's mentor and friend, strongly opposed his sovereign, claiming that clerics could be tried in and punished only by Church courts (where the worst punishment for a criminal act was being stripped of clerical rank and confined to a monastery for life — as opposed to civil hanging!). When most of the English bishops (who did not owe their episcopal appointment to the king as Thomas did) came to oppose his stand against the king, Thomas, in protest, fled to exile in France (1164). Pope Alexander III, himself an exile in France through the Italian invasions of Frederick Barbarossa, was small comfort to the martyr-complexed Thomas. Alexander, who needed no more kingly enemies than he had already, found the Church's champion embarrassing. Finally reconciled with his king, Thomas returned to England in triumph, only to be cut down in Canterbury by some of the king's men. Henry did public penance for Thomas' killing because it was a moment of his rage that had inspired the murder, but his later dealings with the Church were largely untroubled. The conflict over clerics and Church courts was settled by compromise and common sense. And Thomas got what he wanted: martyrdom and sanctification.

Canterbury Cuts Down London Tower

If the English kings considered their bishops to be barons of the realm, the bishops were also fully conscious of their rights and privileges. A case in point is Stephen Langton, archbishop of Canterbury (c. 1155-1228) under King John (1167-1216). Pope Innocent III, a personal friend, named him archbishop in 1207. King John, who had another candidate in mind, refused to accept Stephen, and Innocent excommunicated the monarch. John, faced with barons at home who were murmuring against his excessive taxation, and with the threat of an invasion by King Philip of France to dethrone him, made his peace with the Holy See and became a vassal of Pope Innocent. Stephen landed in England in 1213 and became increasingly sympathetic to the barons who had long resented strong central authority since the days of Henry II. It was the archbishop of Canterbury, baron of the realm, who rallied the other barons to force King John to sign the *Magna Charta* at Runnymede in 1215. The Great Charter, with Stephen's name at the head of the barons signing, became the cornerstone of English law. It guaranteed governmental representation for the more powerful taxpayers of the kingdom; it was the beginning of that evolution of English democracy that terminated in universal adult suffrage in the 20th century. Because he struck a blow for certain liberties due to himself and his fellow barons, the archbishop of Canterbury was removed from his post and recalled to Rome by Pope Innocent. Innocent regarded his friend as a rebel against a king who happened to be the pope's vassal! No pope who feared rebellion in his own city could tolerate a rebellion against one of his vassals. Only upon Innocent's death was Stephen free to resume his duties as archbishop of Canterbury.

If English bishops, as barons, owed fealty to their king, the cases of Thomas Becket and Stephen Langton show that their feudal allegiance did not make toadies of them.

The End of the Roman Honeymoon

When the papacy, to more effectively implement the 11th-century reforms, sent representatives of the popes, (called legates) into a country, thus by-passing the authority of a local bishop and often challenging kingly authority as well, bishops and kings complained. William the Conqueror, Henry I, and Henry II, faithful Catholics all, would permit no communication with the papacy without their permission. In practice this meant that the pope could excommunicate no one without the king's approval. Cases tried in Church courts — and they were many because the Church had jurisdiction over all clerics, crusaders, widows, orphans, and students, and authority over cases dealing with the sacraments, oaths and promises, wills,

sacrilege, blasphemy, to mention only a few — had to be initiated at the lowest level, with Rome recognized normally only as the last court of appeal. Obviously, this was not rebellion against the papacy, but really a safeguard to local Church and state authority.

As the popes in the High Middle Ages became more conscious of their universal authority over the Church, they began the practice of naming bishops to sees outside of the Papal States. (Normally, bishops and abbots were elected to their posts by local officials.) As we have seen, Innocent III named his friend, Stephen Langton, to the archbishopric of Canterbury and aroused the opposition of King John. Robert Grosseteste (1175-1253), the scholarly bishop of Lincoln during the reign of Henry III (1207-1272), went to Rome to protest the number of English bishoprics held by Frenchmen and Italians. (Seven out of 17 sees were held by foreigners who paid a cleric to rule in their place and to send them the bishop's share of the see's income.) This same Robert Grosseteste was none too popular in Rome when he, in the spirit of Stephen Langton, organized an English baronial revolt to maintain the *Magna Charta* against the ambitions of Henry III. The papacy backed its vassal, the king, and the Church in England resented it.

Running the papacy was expensive, particularly when it took on the aspects of a national state at war with its neighbors. The parishes of the papal nation paid ordinary taxes to the Holy See. But the popes also derived income from vassal states. William the Conqueror renewed the old English custom of paying Peter's pence and his successors paid a yearly feudal tribute to their papal overlord. Monasteries directly under the protection of the Holy See paid for that privilege. A newly appointed bishop sent his first year's income to the pope. In 1238 Pope Innocent IV laid a sizable tax upon the Church in England to pay for his war against Frederick II. In 1250 Innocent demanded that the English Church put all of its revenues at the disposal of Henry III who had promised to go on crusade. This constant demand for money soured enthusiasm for the see of Peter among Englishmen — clerics and laity alike.

Opposition to foreigners filling English bishoprics and draining English money from the island continued into the 14th century. In 1351, when England was at war with France and French popes ruled the Church from the exile of Avignon, Edward III (1312-77) passed the statute of provisors that forbade papal appointment of clerics to English sees. In 1353 all appeals to Church authorities outside of England were prohibited by the statute of *praemunire*. The English feared that Church money was going to Avignon to find its way into the coffers of the nation's enemy, the king of France. Though these statutes were rarely enforced, all the legislation necessary to cut the English Church from Rome was on the books almost two centuries before Henry VIII was born. Henry put it to effective use in the 16th century. That he did so without widespread opposition aptly attests to the growing English antipathy toward the papacy during the Middle Ages.

The French Husband of the Church

In France the marriage of the reformed Roman Church and the uneasy French crown was turbulent. The kings reigned over a dynasty where many of their vassals were more powerful than the crown. In the 12th century the dukes of Normandy, who were also English kings, commanded more of France than the Capetian kings. The monarchy came from the area of Paris and had little or nothing in common with its vassals of the south in Aquitaine, Toulouse, and Gascony. Achieving national unity was a work of centuries — and the centralized Roman Church played a major role in that endeavor.

More easily than in England, the reforming popes of the 12th century ruled the French Church through legates. Probably because the French monarchy was weak, communication with Rome was easier. A growing number of monasteries were wards of the Holy See and escaped the authority of the local bishop. When the monks of Mont-Saint-Michel, on the Norman coast, wanted to open a new cemetery, they applied to Rome for permission. More and more, Rome settled disputes between French bishops. Guy of Vienne (the future Pope Calixtus II) was told by the papal legate, Bishop Hugh of Lyons, to stop interfering in the affairs of the monks of St. André-le-Bar. The reformed Roman Church in France was strong — and often strongly resented.

When King Philip I (1052-1108) refused to give up his adulterous union with Bertrada, the countess of Anjou, Pope Pascal II excommunicated the monarch and temporarily stopped the Church from performing its sacred functions in France. The French people, without Mass and confession, forced Philip to see the error of his ways, and the king worked out a settlement of his marital affairs that satisfied the pope. Pascal then entered an alliance with the repentant French king against the emperor, Henry V. *Et voilà* ... the uneasy marriage of Church and state.

King Philip II (1165-1223) greatly expanded the power of the French crown. Pitting his sons against their father, Philip gravely weakened Henry II's hold on Normandy. In 1213, with the cooperation of the papacy, Philip threatened an invasion of England to depose the excommunicated John I. By his victory at Bouvines (1214), Philip drove the English out of northern France. The French king's continental victories so disgusted the English barons that they were able to impose the *Magna Charta* upon their disgraced King John.

Though Philip II personally played no role in the crusade against the heretics of Albi (a group of individuals who were against life and anything that propagated it, such as marriage), he encouraged northern French knights, under Simon de Montfort, to carry out the crusade commanded by Pope Innocent III that proved so profitable in expanding the French monarchy into the southern provinces (1203-1226).

Philip's personal marital problems put him at odds with the pope's legates in France, but he, too, was able to settle them to Pope Innocent's satisfaction to the point where he could ally himself with the papacy in sponsoring young Frederick II for the imperial crown.

A Saint Confronts a Pope

King St. Louis IX (1214-70) was happily married to Marguerite of Provence so his private life caused no embarrassment to the papal legates of the reformed Church. Though much of his life was spent in unsuccessful crusading, as a king and a man Louis was a success. He negotiated peace with England and brought royal justice into his expanded domains. As a saintly king, he was an exemplar of his faith and an effective ruler. Always respectful of the papacy, Louis was not a papal lackey. He refused to recognize Innocent IV's deposition of Frederick II and tried, unsuccessfully, to bring about a reconciliation between the emperor and the pope. In 1247 St. Louis objected to Innocent IV's taxation of the French Church for the war against the Hohenstaufens, and he complained about the number of Italians that the pope appointed to French ecclesiastical jobs.

When the patriarch of Jerusalem became pope as Urban IV (reigned from 1261-64), a Frenchman wore the papal tiara. Without a Rome to call his home, for the Hohenstaufens had seized the Papal States in 1258, Urban regained the Eternal City and concentrated his strategy on reoccupying Northern Italy. After two years of negotiation with St. Louis of France, the pope was able to convince the reluctant king that his brother, Charles of Anjou, should seize the south of Italy from the Hohenstaufens. Louis had not gone along with the pope's deposition of the Hohenstaufens, but he came to see that the south of Italy would make an excellent crusading base. Charles took the Norman Kingdom of Sicily and crushed, once and for all, imperial dreams of a united Roman Empire. The Church in France paid for Charles' Sicilian conquest.

When a French King Beat Up a Pope

When, in 1282, the Sicilians, probably aided by Aragon and Byzantium, rose against Charles of Anjou, King Philip III (1245-85) tried to aid his uncle by attacking Aragonese holdings in the south of France. Pope Martin IV (1210?-1285) permitted Philip to tax the Church of France to pay for the expedition.

King Philip IV (reigned 1285-1314), at war with most of the kingdoms of Europe, levied taxes on the French Church at will. Edward I of England (1239-1307), at war with France, also taxed the English Church with gay abandon. Pope Boniface VIII (1235?-1303) who pictured himself as the king of all kings, threatened with excommunication any king who would tax the Church without the pope's permission. Philip, a wily ruler, unleashed a propaganda campaign against Boniface, accusing him of heresy. He forbade the exportation of gold, munitions, and horses out of France, seriously weakening Boniface's position in his struggle to maintain the Papal States. In a national council held in 1303, Philip called for a general council to condemn a false pope. On September 8, 1303, some of Philip's agents, allied with the powerful Colonna family, who hated Boniface, attacked the pope's residence at Anagni and so abused the pontiff that he died six weeks later.

Pope Benedict XI (reigned 1303-04) calmed the troubled waters by accepting Philip's apology for an outrage that had aroused Christian opinion against him. In return, Benedict allowed a special taxation of the French Church to help bolster France's debased coinage.

When a French pope, Clement V, decided to take up temporary residence in Avignon because he was unsafe in the streets of Rome, Philip IV was delighted. He felt like it would be having a pope as chaplain in his own backyard. The "temporary residence" endured through 7 French popes and 73 years.

The Crusader's Bride

The county-sized Christian kingdoms — Navarre, Castile, Aragon, Portugal — that gradually came into being on the Iberian Peninsula shared one common ideal that shaped their eventual union: the reconquest of the peninsula from the Moslems who had invaded it in 711. Since the breakdown of the Roman Empire in the 6th century, Catholic bishops were often not only religious leaders but civil authorities as well. As the Christian kingdoms evolved and combined through marriage or treaty and expansion into Moslem territory, the Church's bishops supplied more than their share of leadership in the reconquest of Iberia. It was hard to distinguish a bishop from a baron.

In the second decade of the 10th century, the religious reforms of Cluny made themselves felt in Iberia. But in this hodgepodge of crusading kingdoms, where bishops and barons, and even townspeople, were often as freewheeling as kings, the Church seemed far less dependent upon Rome. Rome entrusted much authority to local Iberian officials. It is only in the opening years of the 14th century, when Aragon — a growing Mediterranean menace to, but also vassal of, the Papal States — became involved in the Kingdom of Sicily, that the Iberian marriage of Church and state became somewhat rocky. The popes preferred French to Aragonese neighbors in Naples. And they fought, fruitlessly, for some 20 years to keep it that way.

In 1492 Ferdinand and Isabella drove the last Moslems from Granada back to Africa. The reconquest was complete and the marriage of Aragon to Castile (in the persons of these two monarchs) bespoke a united Spain. Ferdinand and Isabella, given sweeping powers by the popes to reform the Church in a new Spain, emphasized educational and spiritual formation of the clergy in universities. They endeavored to change the image of bishop as baron. Fortunately, due to a prospering middle class, there were numerous churchmen who were not nobles and who portrayed bishops as shepherds of men, not cattle barons.

The problem of the Church in Western Europe was a problem of identity crisis. What exactly was a bishop's job? To whom was he responsible and for what? The close involvement of high ecclesiastics in affairs of state — an involvement inevitable when one considers the importance of Church land in an agrarian society — tended to detach them from the landless poor, and from the landless city dweller who created wealth from craft and commerce. As both nobleman and churchman, the bishop wore two hats — and often suffered the migraine of conflicting loyalties that endangered the loss of his one episcopal head to Church or state.

Discussion Questions

1. Why should churchmen and merchants be the natural allies of national governments as opposed to local strongmen?

2. Why would feudalism, lodged in an agricultural society, inevitably involve churchmen in politics?

3. Why did Innocent III oppose Stephen Langton and the *Magna Charta*? Does his loyalty to feudal obligations betoken future resistance to democratic revolution?

4. How did the French king, Philip II, use Christ's Church to extend the boundaries of his domain?

5. How did the leaders (popes and bishops) of Christ's fragile fellowship suffer an identity crisis during the Middle Ages?

Chapter 10
The Avignon Papal Crisis:
Shepherd or King?

---------------Some of Christ's Fragile Fellowship---------------

Dante (1265-1321) — patriot, protester, poet to the ages.
Jean de Meung (fl.c. 1280) — *Roman de la Rose:* from the
sublime to the earthy in one easy generation.
Bridget of Sweden (c. 1303-1373) — wife, mother of eight,
religious pioneer, seer of visions, pope's pathfinder to Rome.
Gerard Groote (1340-1384) — religion for the middle-class man
on the street.
Geoffrey Chaucer (c. 1340-1400) — faithful critic of the
establishment.

Between 1100-1304 — 204 years, all told — the popes lived
outside of Rome 122 years and spent only 82 years in the
Eternal City. So, the 70-some-odd years the popes passed at
Avignon (1304-77) were nothing unusual. Yet, the fact that the
successors of Peter were refugees from the See of Peter throughout most of the High Middle Ages indicates an identity crisis.
Who were the popes? Were they vicars of Christ, shepherds of
men leading them to the kingdom of God, a religious commonwealth that begins in time but culminates only in eternity? Or
were they rulers of a national state, lodged in the center of the
Italian Peninsula, who vied with emperors and kings in the use
of political power and who frustrated every effort to restore
Rome to either its republican or imperial glory? All too many
Germans and Italians saw them in the latter role and that was
why the popes could not reside in the See of Peter. The city was
unsafe for popes who wanted to be kings. Though — after much
turmoil that involved the chaos of the Protestant Reformation
— the popes eventually regained Rome, the crisis of their role
in the world was only settled in the 20th century when the
papacy abandoned its political ambitions and concentrated

solely upon leavening society with the spiritual ideals of Jesus Christ.

When the archbishop of Bourdeaux, Bertrand de Got (1264-1314), became Pope Clement V in 1305, he decided to rule the Church from the French town of Avignon. (In 1348 Pope Clement VI will buy the city for the papacy). The feuding Orsini and Colonna families made the streets of Rome a jungle, and the Italian Peninsula was a battlefield bathed in the blood of Ghibellines (those who wanted a restored Roman Empire) and Guelphs (those who fought for the national independence of several Italian states, including the Papal States). Clement V, a friend of the French King Philip, established the tone of the Avignon papacy. In dissolving the religious order of the Knights Templar (Council of Vienne, 1311) Clement danced to the tune of the French king who coveted the order's wealth. As time went on, most of the cardinals who advised the pope were Frenchmen and all eight Avignon popes were French. For all practical purposes, the Avignon papacy was Francophile.

Tightening the Reins

On the other hand, sympathy for France never allowed the Avignon popes to lose consciousness of their role as universal heads of the Roman Catholic Church and rulers of the troubled Papal States.

The popes of Avignon centralized authority in the Church by directly filling vacant sees in much of Christendom with bishops they appointed rather than leaving that task to local ecclesiastical election. This was economically profitable for the papacy because the popes received an offering for the vacant see and the first year's income of the newly appointed bishop. By this reservation of Church appointments, among other devices, Pope John XXII (reigned 1316-34) was able to enhance the papal treasury from 12 to 20 million gold francs. While this practice made bishops and abbots of people who were loyal to the Holy See, it also meant that many were absentee landlords, paying a local cleric to do their job while they resided at Avignon or elsewhere, living off the income of a foreign diocese or monastery. This practice of papal appointment angered the local nobility and/or local churchmen who previously had had the privilege of appointing or electing high ecclesiastical officials of their own.

In 1336 Pope Benedict XII defined, for the whole Church's belief, that the souls of the just see the beatific vision imme-

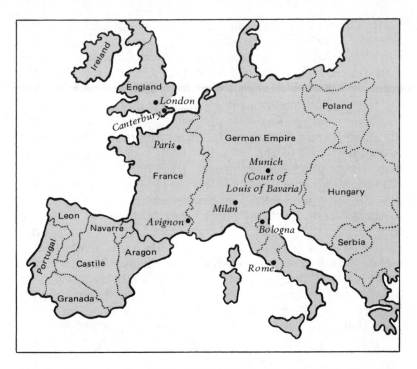

diately upon death rather than having to wait until the resurrection of the body, as his predecessor, John XXII, had mistakenly mused (John was a better economist than a theologian, and his private sermons had opened him to a charge of heresy in several quarters).

Roman Reconquest

While residing in Avignon, the popes never forgot their real home in Italy and they bent every effort to wrest Rome from the jaws of the dogfighting Orsini, Colonna, and Savelli families. In May 1347, Cola di Rienzo (c. 1313-54), the son of a Roman innkeeper, with the connivance of Clement VI and the people of the city, proclaimed himself tribune and put down the squabbling families. But, as far as Avignon and the Roman populace were concerned, his cure was worse than the disease. His luxurious life lost him Roman loyalty, and Pope Clement suspected his territorial ambitions in Italy. Rome's powerful families, this time aided by Avignon, drove Rienzo from the city in December 1347.

In 1350 Pope Clement made Gil Álvarez Carillo de Albornoz (1295-1367), the self-exiled archbishop of Toledo, a cardinal.

Pope Innocent VI (reigned 1352-62) found this successful Spanish Moor-fighter (Albornoz had been papal legate in a winning crusade against the Iberian Mohammedans) just the man to reconquer the Papal States. And he was. In 1354 Cardinal Albornoz handed Rome back to the popes. By 1355 the fighting cardinal brought papal law and order to the States' northern frontier. Raised in the middle-class tradition of the Christian Iberian Peninsula, Cardinal Albornoz insisted upon strong allegiance to the Holy See while recognizing the legitimate rights of city governments. He restrained the privileges claimed by powerful Northern Italian families and, in the end, this was his undoing. Because he refused to hand over Bologna to the Visconti family of Milan, Pope Innocent VI, intriguing with the Viscontis, discharged the cardinal. But not before this Iberian man of genius was able to bring some semblance of legality to the Papal States through his Egidean Code, a codification of laws that endured until 1816. Later reemployed by the papacy, Albornoz made it possible for Pope Urban V (reigned 1362-70) to return to Rome and rule there until 1370 when civil strife forced him to flee to the safety of Avignon.

Paradox of Reform

How ironic it is to consider that the papacy's courageous efforts to reform the Church in the 11th century carried within them the germs of a near-fatal malaise. Seeking independence from powerful lay influence upon ecclesiastical office, the papacy became a national political power, involving itself in deadly warfare with Italian, German, and Aragonese neighbors. This preoccupation with national survival, in its turn, aroused the ire of Catholics, lay and clerical, who lived outside the papal court. They resented the strong centralizing power of the See of Peter decked out in all the panoply of the Norman crusader rather than the homespun seamless robe of Christ. And they could visit their resentments upon all churchmen, but particularly upon bishops and abbots, who, by their style of life, seemed to reflect the worldly ambitions characterized by the Papal States' struggle to survive.

In the 11th century the papacy recognized that there were churchmen who were lustful and greedy for earthly treasure. The popes of that period felt that one way to purge the Church of such clerics was to keep ecclesiastical jobs out of lay hands. Men like Gregory VII called for the personal reform of priests and bishops. Laudable as were their ambitions, often these reforming popes and their advisers (more particularly the latter) encouraged a type of Church reform that was a dagger poised to thrust at the heart of the Church.

The Heresy of Reform

The new wave of barbarian invasions, the breakdown of Charlemagne's empire at the end of the 9th century, the chaotic state of the papacy when powerful Roman families made a toy of it in the 10th century very nearly spelled the end of Christian civilization in the West. Stripped of leadership and discipline, priestly morale and morals crumbled. Anselm of Baggio, talking about Italy, said, "All the priests . . . have wives." Ratherius of Verona (c. 887-974) quipped that if the Church tried to enforce laws deposing married priests, all the priests of Verona would have to pack up and leave. But the Church tried to enforce priestly reform, particularly the strong new popes of the 11th century. The Synod of Rome (1074) forbade priests who fornicated to say Mass. Christians were not allowed to attend a Mass said by a priest who had a mistress. Pope Urban II condemned priests' concubines to slavery, and he and Calixtus II declared priests' marriages to be null and void.

Necessary and well intentioned as these papal reforming measures may have been, they were, nonetheless, dangerous, because they seemed to make the intrinsic supernatural value of the Mass and sacraments depend upon the worthiness of the particular priest administering them. This attitude left the door open to a Puritanism the Western Church had coped with in Africa in the 4th century . . . a heresy called Donatism. And it set the tone for most heretics in the Middle Ages.

Ironically enough, most medieval heretics (with the exception of the Albigensians who were converts to a Middle-Eastern pagan form of nihilistic Manicheism) were would-be Church reformers just one step ahead of the popes in fanatic zeal. Tanchelm of Utrecht, who was stabbed to death by a priest in Antwerp in 1115, taught his followers that sacraments administered by married priests were of no avail. From that point, he arrived at the conclusion that sacraments, especially Matrimony, were valueless signs perpetrated upon society by parasites called priests and bishops who served no purpose for their existence. His 3,000 or so followers at Utrecht, Antwerp, Cambrai, and Liège were so devoted to him that they used to drink his bathwater.

Eon of Stella (d.c. 1148), a new Messiah of 12th-century

Brittany, denied the use of sacraments and the need of the Church itself.

Peter of Bruys (d. 1126?), who taught in Languedoc in the 12th century, railed against sacraments, priests, and the Church as useless and ripe for destruction.

Two Men Who Were Poor

Peter Waldo (d. 1217), a wealthy middle-class merchant of Lyons, was so impressed by Christ's words, "If you seek perfection, go, sell your possessions and give to the poor . . . ." that he gave away all his money and recruited some followers to form "the poor men of Lyons," later called Waldensians. Preaching poverty with their lives, Waldo's disciples denounced the wealth of the Church. Pope Lucius III condemned these would-be reformers in 1184. Waldo's people created their own Church, devoid of sacraments and priests, based upon the Bible. Despite harsh persecutions throughout the Middle Ages, Waldo's followers survived in France, Northern Italy, and Bohemia, where they swelled the ranks of John Hus' heretics and were ready to aid and abet Martin Luther when he appeared upon the scene some 300 years after Peter Waldo.

An Italian contemporary of Peter Waldo, who was definitely making it as the son of a wealthy cloth dealer, was Francis. Bernardone (1181-1226) of Assisi. Like Waldo, Francis gave up his wealth to preach the word of God to the poor. Unlike Waldo, Francis did not flaunt his love of the Lady Poverty to the embarrassment of the Church. He and his followers, "little brothers" (friars minor), lived a rule of life based upon the Gospel and enjoyed the approval of no less a pope than Innocent III.

Francis, deeply in love with God and all his creation, was indeed a beautiful person. For some people, meeting him was like meeting Jesus, so warm was the simplicity of "the little poor man." To many he was the Messiah, but he remained a deacon all his life because he considered himself unworthy of the priesthood. No more a Puritan than his Master, Francis sought to spread good by his example, not by ranting against Church authorities.

The New Spiritual Church

During the 13th century, his Order of Friars Minor flourished in the Church, producing holy men like St. Bonaventure and St. Anthony of Padua. Dedicated to absolute personal and corporate poverty, the Franciscans spread, but success made it very difficult to live up to the letter of this ideal. Some Franciscans felt that owning property was necessary to sustain the order's work. Others would settle for nothing less than the ideal. In 1317-18 Pope John XXII authorized the friars to own corporate property. Certain Franciscans felt this a betrayal of Francis' ideal and they bolted the order. Calling themselves Spirituals (reminiscent of Puritan), they left the Catholic Church in protest.

Near the middle of the 13th century, the Spirituals came into contact with the philosophy of Joachim of Flora (c. 1132-1202). Joachim, a Cistercian monk, had taught that there were three dispensations in the working of human salvation: the order of those bound by the law was the age of the Father's Old Testament; the second age, called the order of clerics, was the era of the Son and rule by the Church; the third and final dispensation, that Joachim thought would begin around the year 1260, was the era of the monks, who would replace the structured Church and create the new Church of the Spirit. The Spirituals saw themselves as Joachim's new spiritual men, destined to shape the new Spiritual Church. Roundly condemned by the Avignon papacy, these separatist Spirituals found refuge in the court of the German emperor, Louis of Bavaria, who was at odds with the Holy See. From the safety of Louis' court, they unleashed a propaganda campaign against the Avignon papacy and particularly against John XXII, the "heretic" whom they wanted an ecumenical council to condemn.

Blueprint for a Middle-class Church

A fellow refugee with the Franciscan Spirituals at the court of Louis of Bavaria was the former rector of the University of Paris, Marsilius of Padua (c. 1275-1342). Though not a Spiritual, Marsilius suffered exile at the hands of John XXII for a blueprint of Church reform that he had drawn up called *Defensor Pacis* (1324). The Church of the new age, according to Marsilius, should be totally under the control of the state. The people, as the source of the state's power, should be the directors of the Church. The only function of the Church was to offer Mass and administer the sacraments. And the people should be the ones to choose who would be priest and bishop. An ecumenical council, composed of priests and laymen, should rule the Church, not the papacy that had come into existence by a fluke of history. The Church should be vowed to poverty. It should be stripped of its lands, and the state should pay priests' salaries.

Marsilius' middle-class, democratic ideas were far in advance of his medieval lifetime, and it is little wonder that Pope Clement VI called him the "greatest heretic of the age." But his heresy descended from a long line of Church reformers who came to believe that the only way to cure the Church was to kill it. And Marsilius, who would enjoy good press in the first quarter of the 16th century, was the wave of the future.

In January 1377, Pope Gregory XI returned to Rome. Largely at the behest of St. Catherine of Siena (1347 [1333?]-1380), the pope returned to Italy to bring peace. Florence, smarting under the French occupation, had instigated popular uprisings in Northern Italy and the Papal States. St. Catherine felt that only a return of the popes to their native city could quell the people's discontent. Pope Gregory became a peacemaker, but his death in March 1378 set the stage for a tragedy in papal history that very nearly destroyed the Church.

Discussion Questions

1. How did the Avignon popes centralize the authority of the Catholic Church?

2. When Cola di Rienzo proclaimed himself "tribune" of the Roman people, what Roman aspirations was he playing upon? What problem did this imply for the Roman papacy?

3. How did Cardinal Albornoz' middle-class upbringing involve him in conflict with powerful Italian aristocratic families? How did his attitude reflect his Iberian background?

4. How can reform become a heresy? Is this possible in the present generation of Christ's fragile fellowship?

5. Why was Marsilius' of Padua *Defensor Pacis* a middle-class manifesto to the Church? How is it a herald of the second Reformation in the 16th century?

Chapter II
Two Popes Too Many

———————— Some of Christ's Fragile Fellowship ————————

Vincent Ferrer (1350-1419) — Jews, flagellants, and Avignon popes.
Giovanni de Medici (1360-1429) — Florentine banker and bosom buddy of the first John XXIII.
John Bessarion (c. 1400-1472) — taught the West Greek.
Nicholas of Cusa (c. 1400-1464) — foursquare religion and relativity.
Michelangelo (1475-1564) — frenetic genius of a fighting pope.

On January 17, 1377, Pope Gregory XI came home to Rome to stay. By the end of March 1378 he was dead.

The French cardinals, the Church's Avignon legacy, gathered together to elect a new pope. Strongly pressured by the Roman populace to elect a Roman, the Frenchmen compromised and elected a Francophile Italian, Bartelemeo Prignano, the archbishop of Bari, who took the name Urban VI. But Urban, resentful of French cardinals not of his making and, perhaps, touched with madness, managed to make life miserable for his papal princes. In a matter of months the cardinals deserted Rome for Anagni where they declared Urban's election invalid due to the menace of the Roman crowd; then they elected Cardinal Robert of Geneva as Clement VII. (Though Urban may not have been quite all there, it is hard to accept the cardinals' legal objections to his election; they had, after all, accepted both Urban's papacy and Urban's papal jobs with their emoluments for nearly six months!)

Urban refused to step down and he named a new college of cardinals more to his liking. The French cardinals with their French pope returned to Avignon. Now Christendom had two popes to choose between and they did: The Empire, England, and Flanders opted for the Italian Urban; France, Scotland, Castile, and Naples, among others, were for Clement. Since both popes excommunicated each other and their followers, there was hardly a Christian in Europe who escaped the ban! Queen Joanna of Naples, by intrigue and force of arms, tried in vain to dislodge Urban from Rome on behalf of her pope, Clement. On the other hand, Henry Despenser, bishop of Norwich, led a disastrous English crusade into French Flanders on behalf of his pope, Urban, and aroused the ire of both the English parliament and the English heretic, John Wycliffe, for his trouble.

Nor were Catholics divided simply along national lines. Within a given country, parishes were often split in their loyalties either to Rome or Avignon; religious orders divided over which allegiance to render, and officials in a given bishopric caused chaos in their personal support of rival popes. If financial support of one papal court had been burdensome, supporting two was disastrous and some Christians were often taxed twice to do just that. True, this was not the first time rivals had claimed the papal tiara, but the disturbance of their dispute had been limited both by time and geography. The great

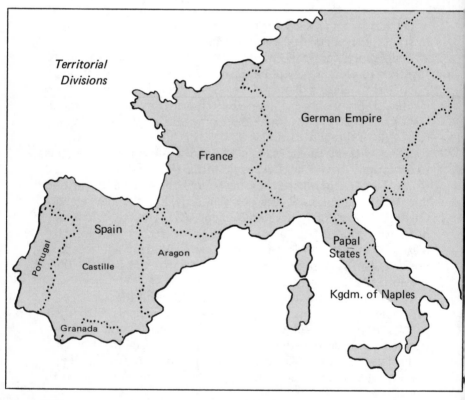

Western Schism, as this event came to be called, divided all of Christendom and endured from 1378 until 1417. The trauma of its final solution was almost as bad as the problem itself, for it haunted the papacy well into the 19th century.

How Do You Get Rid of a Pope?

What was the solution to one pope too many? Really, there was nothing in Church law to cover such a situation. Had one of the popes been willing to resign, the schism would have ended, but neither Urban nor Clement — nor their successors — were quitters, so the breach simply widened with each passing year.

As we have seen, revolutionary churchmen who thought the whole structure of the Church should be changed were plentiful. Peter d'Ailly (1350-1420), an adviser to Benedict XIII (Avignon line, 1394-1423), felt that the real power in the Church was the bishops, instructed by theologians and Church lawyers. Meeting in a general council, they could settle the schism. John Gerson (1363-1429), a Parisian theologian who wrote a book of guidelines for Christians living in a divided Church (he urged the clergy and laity of each pope to pray, accept each other's sacraments, and be charitable in judgment), taught that a general council made up of bishops and theologians had supreme power in the Church. Like d'Ailly, he felt only a council could remedy the schism. John Wycliffe (c. 1329-1389), a priest and theologian of Oxford University, taught that "lordship" depended upon grace. Since the Church of the Western Schism was sinful and disgraced, it had no power to rule and all its property should be confiscated. This kind of teaching pleased the English King Richard II and his nobility until the English peasants in 1381 rose to claim their deserved "lordship" over Church property. The would-be crusader, Bishop Henry Despenser of Norwich, put down the rebellion with great violence, and John Wycliffe went out of style because of his disturbing effect upon the peasantry. Wycliffe effectively denied the need of sacraments and made the Bible the sole source of faith. His teachings, when they were fashionable at Oxford, spread to Bohemia and the University of Prague, where they were strongly supported by John Hus (c. 1369-1415) and his revolutionary followers.

In an effort to end the schism the French bishops withdrew their allegiance from Avignon for 5 years, beginning in 1398. Neither Clement VII (1378-94) nor his successor, Benedict XIII, resigned.

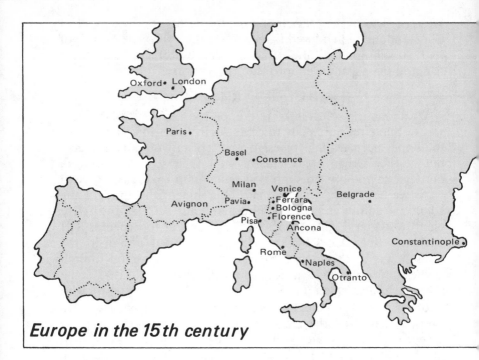

Europe in the 15th century

Then There Were Three . . . !

When the Roman pope, Innocent VII, died in 1406, the cardinals gathered at Rome to elect his successor. Each swore that if elected he would contact Benedict XIII at Avignon to negotiate a mutual resignation of both papacies. Gregory XII (1406-1415), upon his election, contacted Benedict who seemed interested in the plan. But the long dickering over a place to meet indicated Benedict's reluctance to resign the papacy, and Gregory's relatives talked the Roman pontiff out of surrendering his tiara. The cardinals of both papal persuasions, disgusted with the dilly-dallying, abandoned their respective popes, and met at Pisa in 1409. Here they proclaimed that a general council is above a pope and that a council is permanently necessary to govern the Church. The Council of Pisa deposed both Gregory XII and Benedict XIII and elected Alexander V as the new pope. But, since neither the Roman nor the Avignon pope recognized the authority of the council, the Church now had three popes — two popes too many!

Alexander V died in 1410 and Baldassare Cossa, an ex-military mercenary of unsavory reputation, became John XXIII.

The Holy Roman emperor-elect, Sigismund of Hungary — troubled with the revolutionaries of John Hus whose radicals, known as the Wycliffite peasants, would want to confiscate all Church property and take it over for themselves — was anxious to bring an end to the Western Schism. Because of this threat to the existence of Church and state, he pushed the reluctant John XXIII into calling a council at Constance in 1414. John was reluctant because there were ugly rumors that he had bought the papacy. But Ladislaus of Naples had driven him from Rome and the defeated third pontiff needed the emperor as much as the empire needed the council.

The Council of Constance

Peter d'Ailly and John Gerson were the leading lights of the council. Under their inspiration the council proclaimed itself to have a universal authority over the Church that came directly from God and bound every Christian, even the pope. The council's first business was to end the Western Schism. On May 29, 1415, it deposed John XXIII on the equivalent of ecclesiastical "high crimes and misdemeanors." Pope Gregory XII now resigned voluntarily. His rival, Benedict XIII, refused to resign, but the council deposed him in 1417. At last popeless, the council was able to elect Martin V to the papacy in November 1417. The Western Schism was over, but it was up to the new pope and council to bring reform to a shattered Church.

To effect such reform and prior to electing Martin, the council had attacked all would-be reformers in the person of John Hus. But the largely vindictive execution of John Hus as a heretic added little luster to the assembly at Constance. Hus' ideas of reform and those of his English mentor, John Wycliffe, were investigated and condemned. John Hus, attending the council under the protection of a safe-conduct issued by the emperor, never left Constance. Violating the safe-conduct (Sigismund wryly observed that the safe-conduct was for Hus' trip to the council — not necessarily his return!), the conciliar Fathers had Hus burned at the stake on July 6, 1415. His followers, not appreciating the emperor's macabre humor, unleashed a religious civil war upon Bohemia that persisted in varying severity until the eve of the Protestant Reformation.

To aid in the reform of the Church, the Council of Constance passed the decree, *Frequens*, that stipulated that another council should be called within 5 years of the termination of the present assembly — a third within 7 years of the second council — and then one every 10 years. Though Pope Martin V was somewhat less than enthusiastic about this legislation that attempted to set up the general council as a more or less permanent fixture in Church rule, after he closed Constance in 1418, he dutifully called the second council that met in Pavia in 1423. The council came to nothing because it, like its fore-runner, Constance, seemed more intent upon imposing reform on the pope than it did upon the bishops who made up the council. Constance had been absolutely necessary to end the Western Schism, but no pope in his right mind was ever going to accept a general council as superior to the Gospel-given Vicar of Christ. When Martin adjourned the council in Pavia, he was not looking forward to the next one to be held in 1431 at Basel.

When an Ecumenical Council Ruled the Church

Though Martin did not live to endure the torment of Basel (he died in 1431), his fears about a coming conflict with the conciliar Fathers were not unfounded. With great reluctance the new pope, Eugene IV (reigned 1431-47), an upright and intelligent Augustinian monk, called for the council to meet at Basel in 1431. The principal subject of the meeting was to be the reunion of the Church of Constantinople with Rome. (The Eastern Empire's very existence was threatened by invading Mohammedan Turks unless crusading reinforcements could be recruited by uniting with the Roman Church.) But the conciliar Fathers were so intent upon imposing their authority over the papacy that they ignored the pope and began to run the Church without Eugene. The council's administration of the Church proved just as costly as the papal — in fact, the Fathers seized all the taxes that formerly had been paid to the pope to run the Church and they heaped upon themselves all the popular resent-ment that accompanied the taxes.

A popular uprising in Rome threw Pope Eugene out of the city and he became an exile in Florence. But after 1434 the discredited pontiff's fortunes began to improve. Prelates, fed up with the conciliar chaos that developed in Basel when that assembly tried to rule the Church, deserted the council and returned to Eugene. Using soldiers of fortune of the stamp of Sforza and Vitelleschi, Eugene regained the Papal States and Rome; and there he won a new powerful ally, Sigismund of Hungary, whom he crowned emperor in May 1434. Seven hundred Greek churchmen and their emperor, John VIII (reigned 1425-1448), negotiated with Pope Eugene rather than with the conciliar Fathers of Basel, thus increasing papal prestige. In September 1437, Eugene challenged the churchmen of Basel by changing that council's location to Ferrara. The remnants of the conciliar Fathers at Basel deposed Eugene as a relapsed heretic in October 1437 and elected Duke Amadeus of Savoy as Pope Felix V in 1440. (Amadeus, a miserly hermit with a wife and four children, was wealthy; in 1442 he deserted the "papacy" of Basel because the job was just too expensive and he formally resigned in 1449.) Christendom was disgusted with schism and most Christians rallied to the pope. But, although the papacy triumphed over the conciliarists, later popes, particularly in the 16th century, never forgot their narrow escape and looked upon a general council more as a menace than an ally.

Florence and the Greeks

The meeting at Ferrara in 1438 was short-lived. The Papal States were at war with the Viscontis of Milan, and Ferrara lay too close to Milan for the pope's comfort. Then plague broke out. Eugene IV, hardpressed for funds to feed his 700 Greeks and their emperor, in 1439 reopened the council at Florence where the Medici family ruled. The Medicis were papal bankers and they could sustain the visiting Greeks with greater facility.

The assembled Fathers hammered out agreement with the Greeks concerning the *filioque* in the Creed, papal primacy, and purgatory. But the agreement came to nothing because Western attempts to drive off the besieging Turks from Constantinople were military disasters. When Emperor John VIII finally returned to his capital, he found his wife dead. Bowled over with grief, he did nothing to enforce the reunion with the West. The Byzantine man in the street wanted nothing to do with the barbarous "Franks" and the empire fell to the Turks in 1453. The ambitious duke of Moscow, Basil II (1415-1462), who belonged to the Byzantine Church of Kiev, a daughter Church of Constantinople, refused to accept the reunion of Florence because he wanted Moscow to become the religious and political center of a new empire, Russia. In 1448 the Russian Orthodox Church abandoned Kiev for Moscow, and to this day it is the guardian of the Byzantine religious experience.

Papal Crusaders and National Guard

When Byzantium (Constantinople), the Eastern bastion of

Christianity, fell to the Mohammedan Turks in 1453, a cry for crusade swelled in papal throats. But the popes called a war and nobody came. True, John Hunyadi (c. 1407-1456), inspired by the fiery Franciscan, St. John Capistrano (1386-1456), stopped the invading Turks at Belgrade in 1456. And both Pope Nicholas V (reigned 1447-55) and Calixtus III (reigned 1455-58) aided the campaigns of Scanderbeg (1403-1467) in Albania against the Turks. Pius II (1405-64), perhaps the most urbane pope of the 15th century, totally appreciated the growing menace of Mohammedanism abuilding in the Balkans, and he died a crusader en route to the fray at Ancona. The Venetians fought a losing war with the Turks (1463-79) for control of the Aegean, but most Italians, particularly in Florence, Naples, and Milan, shed no bitter tears at Venice's defeat. They feared her growing power in the North of Italy. When Otranto fell to the Turks in 1480, Western Christians did not rally to the cross. Bayazid II abandoned the city in 1481, due to his African-oriented policy and the pressure of Pope Sixtus IV.

Crusading had gone out of style in Italy because there was more profit to gain by fighting at home. Cities like Milan, Ferrara, and Florence were ruled by powerful families (the Viscontis, Sforzas, Medicis) who spent most of the 15th century nibbling away at each other's real estate to enhance their own holdings. The Aragonese Kingdom of Naples looked just as inviting to the French as it had in the 13th century when the German Hohenstaufens had owned it. Throughout the exile of Avignon and the turbulence of the Western Schism, cities of the Papal States, even Rome itself at times, cast off their allegiance to the popes in preference for local strongmen or for fear of neighboring city-states, such as Florence or Milan. And so it is, particularly in the closing two decades of the 15th century, that we see the popes return to the role of national monarchs intent upon securing their rule over alienated real estate by force of arms or cash or both — and the arms and cash were frequently in the hands of relatives seeking their own fortunes, alas, at the Church's expense.

The Silencing of Savonarola

All the austerity Pope Sixtus IV had practiced as a Franciscan did not lessen his penchant for favoring his relatives when he acquired the papal tiara. Bent upon regaining cities lost to the papacy in the northern Papal States, Sixtus' policy was to try to buy off the local strongman or, in the last resort, tumble him from power by intrigue or military attack. His nephews, of whom the pope had plenty, were to replace the dispossessed strongmen. In this way Girolamo de Riario became Sixtus' *gauleiter* of the city of Imola. The pope's plot to overthrow the Medicis of Florence failed scandalously when Archbishop Salviati of Pisa was strung up in full pontificals from a window in Florence's Palazzo Vecchio as a conspirator to the murder of Giuliano de Medici.

Pope Innocent VIII (reigned 1484-92) carried on the policy of Sixtus, due largely to one of the latter's ever-present nephews, Giuliano della Rovere (the future Julius II). A good part of his reign was squandered on a war with Naples that crushed papal finances. The pope created Church jobs and sold them to the highest bidder to balance the war-torn budget.

The notorious Alexander VI (reigned 1492-1503) used his son, the sinister Cesare, to liquidate powerful Roman families (the Orsinis and Colonnas — Giuliano della Rovere fled to France to escape the stilettos of Cesare's assassins) and to rule with French support the northern Papal States. One voice crying out against this was that of the Dominican reformer, Girolamo Savonarola (1422-98). Declaring that the wrath of God would come upon the Church because prelates who once had been pure gold with chalices of wood were now men of wood with chalices of gold, Savonarola, the reformer and ruler of Florence, called for a general council to depose Pope Alexander. Overcome by Florentines who resented religious reforms that smacked to them of fanaticism, Savonarola was hanged as a heretic in the marketplace of Florence and middle-class sobriety dangled from a rope.

The Good Shepherd with a Sword

After the short reign of Pius III (1503), Giuliano della Rovere became pope as Julius II (1503-13). A man of military prowess, Julius cleared the streets of Rome of Cesare Borgia's terrorists. Then he mounted a military campaign against France that made the Papal States a power to be conjured with. Allied with Venice, Spain, England, and eventually the Empire and the Swiss Cantons, Julius II once again presented Christendom with the image of the Good Shepherd clad in armor, anxious to do to death his Christian enemies. Louis XII of France (reigned 1498-1515) called a "general council" at Pisa that "deposed" Julius in 1511. But Julius retaliated with the Council of

Lateran V (1512-1517) where he projected a plan to depose Louis XII and give France to Henry VIII of England (reigned 1509-47). Julius died before his plan could be effected. But not before his many wars and the building of St. Peter's Basilica called for the preaching of indulgences that would so offend stout German middle-class men of the stamp of Martin Luther.

Pope Leo X (1513-1521), the scion of the Florentine house of Medici, a cultivated man of the Renaissance who had no personal vendetta against France, sued for peace after the decimation of his Swiss allies at the battle of Marignano. (At this battle a Swiss military chaplain by the name of Ulrich Zwingli, seeing his countrymen, mercenaries of the popes, cut to pieces, became a pacifist and a "Protestant" in the twinkling of an eye.) In an agreement negotiated with Francis I (reigned 1515-47) at Bologna (1516), Leo X allowed the kings of France to name their "people" to all high Church jobs in France. So it was that "king's men" (mainly nobles) ruled the Church of France from 1516 until the French Revolution (a middle-class uprising) rid itself of both king and Church in another twinkling of an eye.

Discussion Questions

1. Can two rival popes legitimately turn Christ's fellowship out of the Church?

2. Should two rivals claim the papacy today, how would the Church select the real pope?

3. What is the relationship of an ecumenical council to the pope?

4. After further investigation, determine whether Savonarola was a saint or a troublemaker among the fragile fellowship.

5. Should Pope Paul VI modernize the Swiss Guards and declare war on Italy to regain the lost Papal States, what would your attitude as an American Catholic be if he called upon the United States for military aid?

Chapter 12
The Middle-class Merchants
of the Second Reformation

Despite the breakdown of political uniformity that came
with the fall of Charlemagne's empire at the end of the 9th
century, the overriding worldview of Western Christendom
perdured. God was the Creator and the Center of the universe.
His were the heavens and the galaxies. He was the Maker of the
world and mankind. The world and the visible universe mirrored
God's greatness and goodness to intelligent human beings.
Because they could know their God, both through creation and
his revelation in the Bible, human beings were meant to praise
him. But not merely to praise him. The Father had sent mankind his Son to be one of them, to die for their sinfulness, and
to rise to new life so that they might rise from death to be
eternally happy with the Father in heaven. This life on earth
was a short pilgrimage for the medieval person terminating in
eternal life in heaven. Most men of the early Middle Ages,
probably because their earthly life was so precarious, were other
worldly in vision. Religion was not a peripheral interest; it was
at the heart of human existence, the reason a man or woman
came into being.

Lacking strong central governments and, therefore, dependent upon local strongmen to defend them upon this earth, the peasant (and his defending overlord as well) on his pilgrimage to heaven relied upon the clerics of the Church to get him there through the Mass, the sacraments, good works, and pious prayers. Despite political fragmentation, there was an enduring order in Christendom based upon a realistic assessment of the early medieval situation. The vast majority of humankind tilled a given plot of soil for food. It was a world of farmers. A small group of wealthy individuals, who could afford to maintain a fortified estate, a horse, a suit of chain mail, a sword, and lance, defended the farmers. These nobles lived to fight and were fed by the farmers for the protection they afforded against barbarians or hostile fellow Christians. Because this brief "vale of tears" was the vestibule to real eternal life in heaven, the farmers also fed churchmen — bishops, priests, monks — whose contribution to society was to pray people to the Father. And there we have the threefold order of feudal Christendom: the Church, the nobility, and the peasantry.

Other-World Vision

To the early medieval man, this threefold ordering of society was a hard-nosed assessment of the rugged world in which he lived. In each independent village of Western Christendom, amid the fields and hovels of the peasants, stood the fortified manor of the local lord and the church. The lord and his fighting men kept law and order as defender, judge, and executioner. The village priest led the pilgrimage to heaven with the Mass, the sacraments, and prayers. And of the two authorities, the Church much more profoundly influenced the peasant's daily life.

The medieval person did not need the Bible to tell him that this life was short, the very vestibule to eternity. About one-third of all babies died before reaching the age of 5. Blanche of Castille (the mother of St. Louis IX of France) lost 4 of her 12 children at birth and 3 others before they were 13 years old. Among the Hungarian aristocracy in the 15th century, men hardly expected to survive their 21st birthday, and, since so many women died in childbirth, their life expectancy was considerably reduced. Most people were old at the age of 35. In Western Europe 45 to 55 percent of the population were under 20 years of age. With life expectancies that would have sounded the death knell of any respectable insurance company, it is little wonder that the medieval person had eternity on his mind.

The Church Was Noah's Ark

To the peasant (and probably 90 percent of the medieval population belonged to the peasantry) who rose to his toil with the sun and sought his bed when it sank, time enough there was for his job, for time was far from money. Church or monastery bells calling monks and people to prayer in the morning, at nones (noon), and in the evening were the Longines or Bulovas of the farmer's day. Bound to the soil, Sunday was the serf's day of rest. The Church filled the year with feast days of obligation, not only to honor God and his saints but to supply rest and recreation for a hard-pressed peasantry. The farmer, working his fields in the open air, found signs of God in all creation. His church, often large enough to house the whole village, was a Noah's Ark of Christians on their way to the Father with every Sunday Mass. Usually unable to read, the peasant and his overlord could study church statuary, wall paintings, and stained-glass windows that constantly reminded him, through signs and symbols of the Bible, of why he was here and where he was going. Is it any wonder that, living in such a religious atmosphere, holy men and women abounded? Religion was at the core of life; and St. Genevieve, St. Edward the Confessor, St. Francis of Assisi, St. Thomas Aquinas, and St. Louis of France — not to mention St. Catherine of Siena and St. Joan of Arc — were only the best of its many advance men and women.

Living the drabbest of lives, grubbing in the soil from sunrise to sunset, the peasant (and his overlord whose life was only slightly more comfortable and no less precarious) of the early Middle Ages (9th to 12th century) willingly brightened his existence by contributing his tithe to put priests into solemn ceremonial robes that reminded him of the riches of God's kingdom where the first will be last and the last will be first. Thousands of unknown farmers and artisans, working over many generations, created, for the glory of God and the joy of humanity, the cathedrals of Chartres, Notre Dame, Cologne, and the crystal jewel box called the Sainte Chapelle.

Philosophy, Handmaid to Theology

In the 11th century Europe enjoyed an increase in population. Forested lands were cleared and swamps filled to accommodate the new people. Many spent their short lives in monasteries or joined the new religious orders called to a life of poverty and the spreading of the Good News. With the swelling of the ranks of the clergy, literacy increased in Europe and education received a new stimulus. Young clerics sat at the feet of philosophers, trained, perhaps, in the monastic schools of Canterbury, Rheims, or Regensburg; and the universities of Bologna, Paris, and Oxford, among others, were born. The Order of Preachers, founded by St. Dominic in 1220-21, and the Franciscans supplied leading theological speculators in the persons of St. Albert the Great, St. Thomas Aquinas, and St. Bonaventure. Aquinas' *Summa Theologica* is the triumph of a seeking, faith-filled mind using the techniques of Socrates, Plato, and Aristotle to squeeze the truth from the Bible

Drawing of Shaftesbury Psalter — mid 12th century. God-centered symbolic rendition of the dead to Christ.

by close rational analysis. Quite unfortunately (and certainly this was not the intent of the Dominican saint), commentaries like the *Summa* often replaced the use of the Bible itself in the education of clerics. Sound linguistic and historical methods were not allied to the philosophical approach to searching the Scriptures; and the scholastic endeavor of the 13th century largely deteriorated into a parroting of St. Thomas or rank rationalism as manifested in the career of Siger of Brabant (c. 1255 - c. 1282).

Go Directly to God

In Meister Eckhart (c. 1260-1327), a Dominican preacher from Cologne, we find a spirit who acknowledged that God utterly transcended any real capture by the feeble human mind. Only by abandonment of sin and a laying bare of the soul to the influences of the Holy Spirit could the human being commune with the divine Being. Eckhart's mystical approach to God strongly influenced Henry Suso (c. 1295-1366) whose *Little Book of Eternal Wisdom* was widely read in the 14th and 15th centuries. In 1518 it was Martin Luther who supervised the first printed edition of the *Theologica Germanica*, an anonymous mystical treatise that mirrored the teachings of Eckhart and Suso concerning God's transcendence, the ineffectiveness of

human works in reaching him, the need of total abandonment to the Spirit to enjoy communion with God. It is interesting to note that this mystical thrust toward God enjoyed its greatest popularity in Christendom when the Church was enduring the affluence of the Avignon papacy and the chaos of the great Western Schism. Was this so because these mystics of the Rhine Valley showed a way to go to God directly without the mediation of the Church?

Sketch from the tomb statuary of Sir Ralph Greene and his wife (d. 1417). Man-centered facing of death with a memorial that they had lived.

Surely this is the way men like Martin Luther, Ulrich Zwingli, and John Calvin used the mystics of the Rhine.

The Anxiety of Occam

William of Occam (c. 1300-1349), a Franciscan philosopher of Oxford, believed the human mind incapable of any knowledge that corresponded to reality and, therefore, incapable of proving God's existence. All one knows of God comes by faith, said William. Since the human mind does not know reality, it really cannot comprehend goodness or evil. Goodness and evil depend upon God's decree and, since the mind cannot know God, what God decrees to be good today, he could decree to be evil tomorrow, the human mind all unknowing. Occam's anxiety-ridden philosophy left little room for the teaching authority of a universal Christian Church and put all its emphasis upon Biblical revelation. It strongly influenced "the merchant's theologian," Gabriel Biel (c. 1420-95), who lauded the

117

storekeeper and financier as useful members of society whose prosperity should be fed by the laws of supply and demand, not diminished by the moralizing maxims of vain philosophy. Biel's and Occam's middle-class, pragmatic, theological outlook were the "scholastic" texts German clerics of young Martin Luther's generation were exposed to. Hence, Luther's utter contempt for scholastic philosophy.

Maverick Middle-class Merchants

Gabriel Biel, "the merchant's theologian," has been called a transitional philosopher because his thinking represented a changing of order in the stratified society of clerics, nobles, and peasants who peopled the Middle Ages. In the old cities of the Roman Empire (particularly in the Italian Peninsula) and in the new cities of Christendom slowly developing at important seaports (that is, Bruges, Genoa, Venice), on important waterways (that is, London, Frankfurt, Cologne), at sites of fairs where peasants exchanged commodities for artisans' wares (that is, Ypres, Troyes, Winchester), a new manner of man made the medieval scene. He was the merchant, the maverick of the

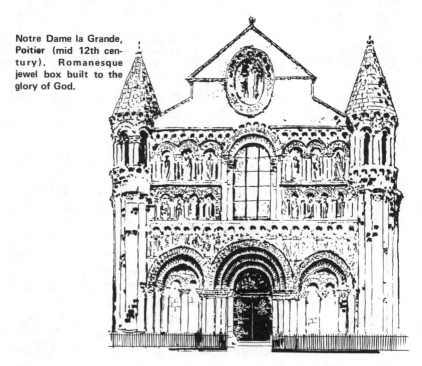

Notre Dame la Grande, Poitier (mid 12th century). Romanesque jewel box built to the glory of God.

Middle Ages. A Catholic, but not a cleric, he did not pray men to God. Affluent, but no fighter, his affluence depended upon peace. He did not grub the soil to make his living; rather, his income came from the skill of his hands in spinning flax into linen or shaping pewter into dinnerware. He transported wine from Bourdeaux to London or wool from London to Bruges. The crusades created a Frankish taste not only for real estate in the Near East but for spices, dates, figs, almonds, and Syrian wines; and more and more merchants there were to cultivate and satisfy this taste. Though looked upon as "the commons," the middle-class man formed a new estate in society, an estate that will seek to dominate history from the 13th to the 20th century.

Man of This World

Artisans and merchants lived together in cities composed of their homes, shops, and warehouses. As they catered to their customers, their incomes increased — permitting a personal indulgence in fine wines, rich foods, soft garments to symbolize their affluence, tapestries to warm the chill of their homes, objects of art to brighten their lives. Not noble by birth, they could buy their way into the nobility by well-endowed marriages. Their wealth bought them immunity from feudal overlords, either lay or religious, and gave them a great deal of independence in running their city in a way that was good for business.

To people who spent their lives in commerce speculating on commodities, time was money and it could no longer be measured by the easygoing chimes in a monastery garden. Precision clocks graced Gothic town halls that competed with cathedrals as architectural wonders. In the later Middle Ages (13th to 15th century) many cathedrals rose less to the glory of God than to the glory of the city's wealthy canons and burghers. Cosmopolitan in their interests, merchants developed a banking system based on credit and promises to pay that liquefied the economy, and money bred money.

For this monied middle-class, life became less precarious than it was for the nobleman and peasant. Brief as it might be, these middle-class people saw that it could be sweet. Far more self-conscious than heaven-conscious, they reflected the value of life on this earth in the realism of Gothic art as contrasted with the primitive theological symbolism of early medieval Romanesque. Funereal statuary that once portrayed man's destiny as either a

Town hall of Ypres (13th century). Grand Gothic emporium built to the glory of man.

permanent citizen of heaven or hell yielded to images of the dear deceased, — men and women who had lived and loved and who had tasted life and had found it good.

Who Needs Priests If You Have the Bible?

No less Catholic than the peasants and nobles, a middle-class man's attitude toward the Church was quite different. Men of business had interests in this world. Just as they sought independence from the local nobility (merchants were often firm allies of kings seeking to create national states), increasingly they tended to resent the spiritual authority of the Church. Building and paying for fine churches and hospitals, middle-class people were willing to accept bishops and priests as their chaplains but not as spiritual overlords. Money bought education; and education, literacy. Middle-class men often favored philosophers like Marsilius of Padua, William of Occam or John Wycliffe who looked upon the clergy more or less as charlatans standing between the people and their God who could be found in the Bible. What Bible-reading Christian needed a priest? Many came to resent the lands and buildings their forefathers had given to the Church. The rich vestments and vessels of the liturgy did not brighten their lives because they themselves wore fashionable clothing suitable to their state, and the vessels of their dinner tables often rivaled the chalices of the altar.

The pageantry of the Church, particularly the Church of Avignon and after, only lightened the merchants' purses as money left England, France, and the Empire to support the papacy. But far from being nonbelievers, these middle-class, medieval men only craved a Church and a state that they could control, not one that controlled them.

Given this preoccupation with the things of this world, one can understand the pessimism that enveloped Western Europe when the Black Death of the early 1350's carried off, in a matter of months, nearly half the population of Christendom. The Western Schism some 20 years later stripped Christians of spiritual leadership in the midst of economic depression, war, and death. For the second time there was a "Christian loss of nerve," the prelude to a second Reformation that would inevitably follow. But this time that Reformation came not from kings or popes but from middle-class merchants and their offspring, the mavericks of the Middle Ages who really could tolerate no authority but their own because they knew the world was theirs.

Discussion Questions

1. If each of us knew that we would barely survive our teen-age years, what effect would this have upon the life style of Americans?

2. After further research, discuss how medieval rationalism has influenced theology in the Church.

3. Through further reading, discuss the role of the medieval merchant as the maverick of medieval feudalism.

4. Discuss the relationship of contemplative prayer with the sacramental and hierarchical structure of Christ's fragile fellowship.

5. Discuss "Christian loss of nerve" related to the Black Death and the Western Schism and compare it to chaotic events in contemporary history, for example, World War II, Vietnam, "the bomb," "population explosion," scarcity, etc.

Chapter 13
Luther and the Church -
the Second Reformation

────────── Some of Christ's Fragile Fellowship ──────────

Adrian Dedel (1459-1523) — the pope who might have out-dated Luther.

John Reuchlin (1455-1522) — Hebrew, the Bible, and anti-anti-Semitism.

Thomas More (1478-1535) — emerging Catholic layman, lawyer, and scholar.

Ulrich von Hutten (1488-1523) — German chauvinism disguised as religion.

Thomas de Vio, Cajetan (1469-1534) — scholastic philosopher turned Scripture scholar.

───

The world of the second Reformation was peopled with willful, creative giants. Michelangelo's *Last Judgment* sets the cosmic tone. Everything was larger than life and charged with change that mounted to frenzy. A sinner and a soldier, Popes Alexander VI and Julius II, spent treasure and shed blood to see that the Papal States would never again be the plaything of German emperors, French kings, or Italian freebooters.

Frustrated in the Italian Peninsula, Francis I sought to make France a Mediterranean power by alliance with the infidel Turk. Just as willfully, Charles V manned the Holy Roman Empire's eastern frontier to stave off Francis' infidel allies who threatened to overwhelm Christendom. In England a new breed of men, gentleman farmers, climbed their way to the top on the coattails of an upstart named Henry Tudor who became the seventh Henry to rule the realm. Fortunes were to be made in commerce. The Medici family, bankers of Florence, supplied a pope to the Church, Leo X, and a queen to France, Catherine de Medici. The Fugger family of Augsburg underwrote many papal projects, not the least of which was the building of St.

Peter's in Rome. In England, wool became the way to wealth and the new landed gentry closed more and more land to the plow to make it available for the pasturing of sheep. Farm laborers, thrown out of work, became an ill-fed, ill-clad, ill-smelling city rabble, the future "hands" of the industrial revolution.

Medieval mysticism and the sterile, senseless philosophy of Occam and Biel set everyday religion upon a course of often frenetic do-it-yourself asceticism (witness the extreme popularity of Thomas à Kempis', *The Imitation of Christ*) and an uncharted pilgrimage of faith derived from the Bible.

The papacy's quest for national security, often reflected in the ambitions of local churchmen overly concerned with the Church's honor and solvency which they identified with their own, left God's pilgrims without the guides they needed on their voyage of faith. Anticlericalism was rife in this new world of commerce and middle-class common sense. The literary giant of the age, Erasmus, poked cruel fun at the foibles of churchmen and even the saintly Thomas More could fire a witty salvo at ambitious and avaricious priests.

The Frenetic Champion of the Second Reformation

A German Augustinian monk, Martin Luther, characterized the frenzy of his age so well that he became the champion of the second Reformation.

Martin Luther was born in 1483 at Eisleben in Thuringia, the son of a miner who worked his way up to manage several foundries and mines in Mansfeld. Young Martin came of good, no-nonsense, middle-class stock. Part of his Latin studies were made at Magdeburg where the Brothers of the Common Life supplied his spiritual direction in the atmosphere of the *Imitation of Christ*. Luther entered the most important university in the empire, Erfurt, around 1499 where his father wanted him to study law. Instead, he studied philosophy at the school of Occam and Biel and graduated as a master in 1505, second in a class of 17. Then, over his father's protests, Luther joined the Augustinians. Ordained a priest in 1507, Luther continued his theological studies at Erfurt and at the new university of Wittenberg where he also taught.

As a young priest Luther led an extremely active life as subprior of the Wittenberg Augustinians, preacher at the collegiate church, and professor at the university. Raised in the asceticism of the *Imitation of Christ* but also schooled in the

NORTH SEA

BALTIC SEA

Magdeburg • Wittenberg Poland
Mansfeld •
• Eisleben

Erfurt

Mainz •
Worms •
Speyer •
Augsburg •
• Munich
Hungary

HOLY
ROMAN EMPIRE

insecurities of Gabriel Biel's philosophy that rendered man incapable of any kind of knowledge of God, Luther turned to the medieval mystics of the Rhine to savor the spirit of self-surrender. He also devoured the Bible and relished the rigorous God-centered writings of St. Augustine.

But Luther's busy life disqualified him as a mystic; and Biel's philosophy of an autocratic God who could call a thing good one day and classify it as evil the next — his creatures all unaware of the Deity's change of mind — left Martin a nervous wreck with scrupulosity. Nothing would be enough for such a God, not even all the religious observances catalogued in the *Imitation of Christ*, even if they were done to the letter.

Luther Discovers God's Mercy

Luther claims that he made his discovery of God's mercy in 1519, but his early writings indicate that it was as early as 1514 that Martin realized that man is saved by faith and confidence in the Father, not by anything he does. No matter what the date, what a healing realization it must have been for a young monk muddling in the neurosis of scrupulosity! Luther discovered that the adventure of living a full Christian life is lodged in the "story of hope," the Bible. God, the loving Father,

125

created human beings to share life on his level and to be perfectly and eternally happy in the possession of him. To assure their salvation the Father freely sent his only Son, Jesus, the God-man, to die for humans, who are fundamentally wicked, and to rise from the dead in their place, thereby meriting for them eternal life.

The Good News, all that really counts in the Bible, is that a human being can become united with the dying and rising Christ and thereby be saved. And this not by frenzied religious asceticism or even by keeping the commandments (a pagan as an integral human being was obliged to keep the moral law, after all), but by firm faith and confidence in the loving Father — one who would indeed redeem his free offer of salvation if man would but cast his whole being into the Being, Jesus Christ, the Victim and Savior. Man had to recognize Jesus as the Lord of his life. His good actions would follow upon his faith, not in frenzy but freely, in cool confidence that it is God who has made him lovable and worthy of eternal life.

Consoling as this teaching must have been, it is hard to see how this was in any way a new discovery. Except for Luther's pessimism regarding the fundamental wickedness of human nature (and here, it must be admitted, writers and preachers of Western Europe, from the time of Augustine [354-430] through the Middle Ages, were less than enthusiastic about human potentiality), the Good News of salvation by faith alone was pretty standard preaching from the days of Gregory I (d. 604) to Martin's own era. And, correctly understood, this remains thoroughly orthodox today. The Council of Trent (1545-1563) decided, only after Luther's death, exactly what the reception of the Good News does to a person internally — a moot point and open to discussion during Luther's lifetime.

Luther Drops the Bomb

It was less Luther's theological outlook and more his hard-nosed, slightly chauvinistic, no-nonsense, middle-class background that got him in trouble with the Roman religious powers that were.

In 1514 Albrecht of Brandenburg (1490-1545) was made archbishop of Mainz and one of the 7 electors of the German Empire (those who voted an emperor into office). He was already bishop of 2 other interesting sees, Magdeburg and Halberstadt. Pope Leo X taxed young Albrecht 14,000 ducats for the See of Mainz, and 10,000 extra ducats for the privilege of being bishop of 3 dioceses at the same time. Jacob Fugger, merchant banker of Augsburg, advanced the money and paid the pope. In return, the new archbishop, for the first time, allowed the papacy to preach indulgences in the electorate in return for money donated to the construction of St. Peter's Basilica (begun in 1503 by Pope Julius II). Though not publicly known, half the proceeds of the preaching was to go to the house of Fugger, the other half to the papacy for the building of St. Peter's.

John Tetzel, a dynamic Dominican speaker, preached the indulgence successfully and correctly, but he was too good a salesman to pass up gimmickry in the aid of his cause. Certain students at Wittenberg enthusiastically called Father Tetzel to the attention of their mentor, Dr. Martin Luther. Luther — discoverer of God's mercy (through faith, not indulgences) and a leading light of Wittenberg — feeling that the Dominican's "pitch" for the indulgences was only slightly less than scandalous, decided to scrutinize the whole doctrine of indulgences in an academic debate.

He drew up the *95 Theses* in a scientific and respectful tone. Counseling respect for the pope and the preacher of indulgences, Luther questioned whether the papacy could spring a soul from purgatory in exchange for a monetary contribution. Good works of charity could certainly aid a soul in purgatory, but was it prudent to pick purses to assure that happy result? A man of the middle class, Luther verbalized with ingenious accuracy hypothetical, but embarrassing, questions which Germans with a little money might put to an Italian pope: "Since the pope's income today is larger than that of the wealthiest of wealthy men, why does he not build this one church of St. Peter with his own money, rather than with the money of indigent believers?" (Had Luther known something about the deal between Albrecht, the house of Fugger, and Pope Leo X, he might have been less respectful!)

That the academic debate ever took place at Wittenberg is unknown. What *is* known is that the *95 Theses*, written in Latin toward the end of October 1517, were spread broadcast by Luther's admirers, and as early as December they were translated into German and became a best seller. Luther, never out of touch with the hardworking people of his class, struck a responsive note in outraged bourgeois hearts. Almost overnight he became, willy-nilly, the champion of Church reform. Protected by the elector of Saxony, Frederick the Wise (who had never permitted the indulgence for St. Peter's in his state), Luther attracted the interest of German patriotic knights like Ulrich von Hutten and Franz von Sickingen (who resented papal opposition to the Holy Roman Empire in the Italian Peninsula) and, eventually, a reforming humanist of the stamp of Erasmus of Rotterdam (c. 1466-1536).

The Song That Became Too High to Sing

But the young Augustinian also made enemies. The popularity of the Dominicans was on the wane (though their general, Cardinal Cajetan, had been close to Julius II and was an adviser to Leo X), and they were anxious to avenge the insults leveled at a fellow follower of St. Dominic by an upstart Augustinian. The *95 Theses* that Luther had framed as questions open to disputation now became, in Dominican hands (and also through his own comments on them), assertions to be condemned as heretical. The Dominicans exerted powerful influence in Rome to have Martin condemned. But Pope Leo X was little alarmed by Luther and was anxious to please Martin's protector, the Elector Frederick, whom he saw as an acceptable successor to the aging Emperor Maximilian I. The wily Medici pope did not want Maximilian's grandson, Charles I of Spain, who had interests in Southern Italy, to be elected emperor — the old Papal States' phobia of a German power dominating the north and south of the Italian Peninsula thus coming to the fore once again. So he handled this "Lutheran" storm in a teacup with kid gloves.

Meanwhile, Luther, pushed along by events and feeling he was losing control — as indicated by his words, " ... For I myself did not know what the indulgences were, and the song threatened to become too high for my voice ... " — did little to pour oil on troubled waters. By the first anniversary of his *95 Theses*, the Augustinian had managed to defy the Dominican papal legate, Cardinal Cajetan, sent by Rome to receive his recantation — " ... He (Cajetan) is about as fit to deal with this as an ass is to play a harp ... " And by the summer of 1519 (when his *95 Theses* had already been translated into French and he was known all over Christendom) Luther had denied the authority of the pope or a general council in religious matters, opting for the Bible as the sole source of faith to be privately interpreted by each individual.

Luther's Middle-class Game Plan of Reform

In August 1520, Luther wrote his *Appeal to the Ruling Class of German Nationality as to the Amelioration of the State of Christendom.* In it he denies any special religious power to priests. All Christians, by Baptism, are priests. Men ordained by bishops, even by the pope himself, are just baptized Christians designated by the community to fulfill a particular function. If a priest is defrocked, he ceases to be a priest. Since people of religion are no different from Christian "tailors, shoemakers, stonemasons, carpenters, cooks, menservants, farmers, and all secular craftsmen . . . " who are subject to the state, so should so-called religious people be subject to the state.

In rather chauvinistic tones, Luther calls upon the German nobility to reform abuses in the Church. He calls for a practical break with Rome by the local election of bishops, one bishop to a see, the ignoring of papal legates, the cutting off of German money flowing to Rome in the form of taxes, stipends, and fees. No cases should be appealed to Rome. The pope should be kept out of temporal affairs, such as his domination of the Papal States. Celibacy should be voluntary as far as priests are concerned. Luther felt celibacy to be unnatural, a gift to a very few. Feast days should be abolished because they only encouraged idleness and drunkenness . . . . " . . . 'Holy days' are not holy, whereas 'working days' are 'holy' . . . . " Universities, reserved for the education of the affluent and noble, needed reform; that "pagan rascal," Aristotle, should be pruned from the curriculum. Priests should be doctors of Holy Scripture and men of few other books.

These were only a few of the changes Luther proposed. Some of them were needful. Luther correctly recalled the priestly role of all Christians, but, in denying any special sacramental character to ordained priests, bishops, and popes, he also implied that the Mass and sacraments were mere signs that did nothing to change or better the People of God in any essential way. Even here, at this point in time, Luther was playing in a theological area open to discussion, since it had not been authoritatively defined exactly what a sacrament did to a Christian internally.

Nevertheless, this strong-minded, even stubborn, Augustinian was playing with fire. His *Appeal* smelled like the *Defensor Pacis* of Marsilius of Padua, and John Hus had gone up in smoke for saying a good deal less. Whether or not Luther was technically a heretic when he issued his *Appeal* to the German nobility, like Peter Waldo, John Wycliffe, and Marsilius of Padua before him, he was definitely rebelling against the Roman

Catholic Church. There was little else Pope Leo X could do but condemn him. Luther was excommunicated in September 1520.

Salvation by Faith, Not Sacraments

In response Luther published *The Babylonian Captivity of the Church*. Luther accused the pope and the priestly caste of holding the Church, the People of God, in thralldom through the sacraments. He again asserts that all Christians are priests. Sacraments are nothing more than signs that any Christian can confect. The pope, priests in general, said Luther, are parasites living on a gullible Christian society through a "con game" called the Mass, not a sacrifice but merely a commemoration of Christ. He quite frankly states that without sacraments no priesthood is necessary and the papal captivity of the Church will end. Any Christian in the Church can be called to the ministry of Christian service that is nothing more, nor less, than the preaching of the word of God. Luther would emphasize the absolute need of the vernacular, in his case, German, in liturgical services, because faith comes through hearing and understanding God's word.

In November 1520, Martin completed his Reformation game plan by publishing his third pivotal treatise, *The Freedom of a Christian*. Luther rightly points out that man is saved by his confidence (faith) in God's promise of a Redeemer; he is saved by a confidence that makes him one with Jesus, much as a bride shares in the total being of the bridegroom. The Christian truly serves his redeeming God by good works that freely flow from his faith. But it is his faith and confidence in the Father and Jesus that saves him, not his works, the fruit of his faith.

Martin warns that there will be those who will misunderstand and act evilly because they will say that good works do not matter. But they will be wrong because they lack total faith in Jesus who performed good works as a man, though he needed no salvation. On the other hand — and here the middle-class medieval anticlerical comes to the fore — they are equally wrong who claim that salvation comes simply from fulfillment of fasts, penances, devotions, and ceremonies. He infers that these latter people — popes, bishops, and priests — have shackled the free Christian with routines of devotion binding him to the Roman Church while they have neglected to teach him that faith and confidence in the Father and Jesus are the lifeblood of their works.

Luther, the Bungling Prophet

To sum up, the reason for Luther's revolt was born of a middle-class resentment of what he considered to be an abuse of ecclesiastical power. He correctly emphasized the priesthood of the People of God to correct abuses rampant among clerics. But, in treating the clergy as charlatans and parasites, he also, unfortunately, destroyed the sacraments, symbolic but vital encounters with Christ that nourish Christian growth in faith and in confidence. This, unwittingly, was a death blow aimed at the Mystical Body of Christ, the People of God. Luther's teaching on salvation by faith alone remains orthodox to this day, though that salvation doctrine was modified and clarified by the Council of Trent after his death.

For all his rebellious spirit, Luther was a bungling prophet of the grass-roots Catholic Church. When the song became too high for his voice, he raucously screamed that the People of God numbered more than the pope, the bishops, and priests among their ranks. Rebel though he might be, he recalled that Christ's Church was a Church of service, not a Church of overlordship. As Cardinal Reginald Pole (1500-1558) was to point out at the Council of Trent, not everything Luther and his followers stood for was wrong.

Discussion Questions

1. How was Martin Luther a prophet to the fragile fellowship?
2. What was Luther's heresy?
3. Does Luther's teaching on salvation by faith alone differ from that of St. Paul?
4. Discuss the theological tenet: All Christians, by Baptism, are priests.
5. Compare Luther's teaching on the Church with that of Marsilius of Padua in his *Defensor Pacis*.

Chapter 14
Luther's Reformation
Becomes Protestant

Some of Christ's Fragile Fellowship

Jacopo Sadoleto (1477-1547) — urbane and gentle reconciler of Protestants.

William Allen (1532-1594) — Catholic martyrs for England and propaganda for Spain.

Marguerite of Angouleme (1492-1549) — influential liberated lady who favored the "new learning."

Margaret Clitherow (c. 1556-1586) — English Catholic convert who was crushed to death for hiding a priest.

John Faber (1478-1541) — "the hammer of the heretics."

Pope Leo X saw the dreaded Charles Hapsburg (Charles I of Spain who ruled the empire from 1519-1556) proclaimed emperor at Charlemagne's imperial chapel in Aachen in January 1520. The fifth imperial Charles, his empire geographically dwarfed the domains of Charlemagne. His empire — composed of Spain, the Low Countries, Germany, Southern Italy, vast areas of South America, Mexico, and lands in North America that swept from Florida to Southern California — was so far-flung that it became his undoing. Charles spent most of his reign as a campaigner fighting to hold Spain in his sway — successfully but at what a cost! He kept France out of Northern Italy — much to the despair of the Papal States who dreaded Germans both in the North and South; and devout Catholic though he was, he sacked Rome in 1527 because Pope Clement VII was the military ally of Francis I, king of France. He worried about his eastern frontier when the Turks laid siege to Vienna in 1529, and he juggled his Catholic conscience in Germany because he could not alienate the core of his empire by stamping out Lutheranism when a host of his imperial German princes were Lutheran and he needed their men and

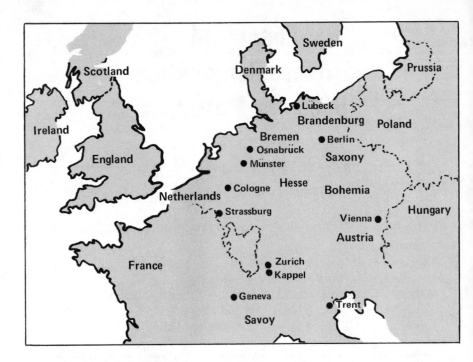

money. Little wonder the harassed Charles gave his brother, Ferdinand, the empire and retired to a monastery 2 years before he died in 1558!

But this was all in the future and only gradually dawning, when the 21-year-old emperor summoned the Augustinian excommunicate, Martin Luther, to the diet (a general imperial assembly) being held at Worms in the opening months of 1521. Luther refused to budge from his theological position, and the emperor, in April 1521, declared him an outlaw. He did, however, grant him a safe conduct back to Wittenberg before anyone in the empire could carry out his right to kill him. En route to Wittenberg the Elector Frederick had his men waylay Martin and spirit him off to Wartburg castle, near Eisenach, where the Augustinian could be guarded from his enemies.

"Prisoner" of the Wartburg

Martin's hidden years at the Wartburg were far from idle. For it was there he translated the Bible into a brand of German that was so dynamic and widely read that it helped to shape a standard language for the empire. His friend, Philip Melancthon (1497-1560), a fellow refugee in the Wartburg, systematized

Luther's theological insights in a practical book of pastoral theology called *Loci communes*. In his two *Catechisms*, Luther developed a down-to-earth method of communicating his teachings to the men and women in the pews, a system that would be put to good use by Roman Catholic imitators, such as the Fathers of the Council of Trent and St. Peter Canisius (1521-97) of the Society of Jesus.

But, if the Wartburg years were fruitful, they were also years of trial and doubt for Martin. The failed Augustinian priest often doubted the righteousness of his stand. And it was at Wartburg that the central weakness of his reform — replacing the authority of the papacy with the private interpretation of the Bible — undermined his middle-class Church. Like Wycliffe and Hus before him, Luther's "new learning" (particularly private interpretation of the Bible and salvation by faith alone) appealed to the social have-nots of the empire who saw it as a means of striking out against all authority, political as well as religious, and of helping themselves to the persons and property of their "betters."

Luther's Fanatic Disciples

In 1522, the German knight, Franz von Sickingen (1481-1523), in the interests of a purely secular empire and the teachings of Martin Luther, attempted to seize the territory of the prince-bishop of Trier; but the archbishop, allied with several princes of the empire, turned the tables on von Sickingen and killed him on the battlements of his own castle at Landstuhl.

The next upstarts against authority in the name of Martin Luther were less aristocratic than von Sickingen, but no less determined. While Luther was in the Wartburg, two of his disciples, Andreas Carlstadt and Thomas Müntzer, stormed into Wittenberg spewing the fire and brimstone of a "hot Gospel." Agreeing with Luther's teaching that all Christians were priests, bearers of the Holy Spirit, and, therefore, free of any organization that cut them off from God, these two fanatics abolished Wittenberg's Mass (something Luther intended to do in the course of time), substituting for it a communal meal eaten by the faithful. They replaced altars with tables, destroyed crucifixes, and hacked statues to pieces. Disagreeing with Luther that Christ was really present in the Eucharist, their people received Communion as a mere reminder of Jesus.

Thomas Müntzer believed that in this world there were only

135

the saved and the damned. The saved were the accepters of his message, and they avoided every form of evil. Anything worldly was evil, whether it be Church ceremonies or taverns, civic affairs or wedding feasts. Not content to let God separate the sheep from the goats, Müntzer preached that it was the duty of the saved to destroy the damned. To be saved a person had to receive Baptism again, because the Baptism that he had received as a child was worthless. According to Müntzer, infants could not freely accept Jesus as their Savior by a conscious act of commitment. This practice of rebaptism of adults earned these rebels the title of Anabaptists — meaning those who baptize again. Both Catholics and Lutherans found this practice shocking.

Luther's "Paper Papacy"

On March 1, 1523, the situation was so desperate that Luther had to leave the Wartburg and return to his pulpit in Wittenberg. Within a week of preaching Luther won back the populace to his gospel, and his fanatic disciples had to leave town. But he lost an old friend in Andreas Carlstadt and made a dire enemy of Thomas Müntzer. Looking upon Luther as a leader of "the synagogue of Satan," Müntzer referred to his former chief as "the pope of Wittenberg" and "Doctor Liar."

The peasants of Suabia, Thuringia, Wesphalia, and Alsace, crushed beneath the burden of feudal taxes and forced labor, marched to the beat of Müntzer's drum and slaughtered both secular and ecclesiastical oppressors. In a pamphlet entitled *Against the Murderous and Thieving Hordes of Peasants*, Luther, staunch ally of law and order, cried, "Let everyone who can, slay, smite, and stab (the rebels) .... "

Carlstadt was dumbfounded at Luther's violence. After all, he and Müntzer and their followers, directly inspired, as they thought, by the Holy Spirit and the Gospel, were simply exercising their freedom as Christian men — a thing Martin had strongly recommended when the Reformation began. Now Luther delivered Christianity from the papacy only to hand it over to the state. For the peasant's revolt in Germany was finally put down, with immense loss of blood, only when Catholic German princes, in alliance with the Lutheran Philip of Hesse, captured the last stronghold of the Anabaptists, Münster, in 1535. Sebastian Franck (1499-1542), an Anabaptist champion of religious toleration, was later to say of Luther that he had made a "paper papacy" of the Bible where the strongest individual interpreter became pope.

Lutherans Become Protestants

Luther's "new learning" of the Gospel spread throughout the empire. Elector John of Saxony became pope of Luther's Church with Martin's blessing. Albrecht of Brandenburg — Ansbach (1490-1568), the last grand master of the Teutonic Knights (a military religious order, like the Knights Templar, created for crusading), turned his order's lands into the duchy of Prussia and became a Lutheran. Philip, the landgraf of Hesse (1504-67), turned Lutheran in the 1520's and founded the University of Marburg for the training of Lutheran theologians. Many northern German cities (such as Minden, Osnabrück, Riga, and the region of Pomerania), with their middle-class merchants, climbed on the bandwagon and received the gospel according to Martin Luther.

In the face of these growing conversions Catholic Emperor Charles V seemed powerless. When he tried to limit Lutheran expansion he found some of his most powerful princes and richest cities in arms against him, ready to *protest* a return to Roman Catholicism with their lives and fortunes. (The name Protestant stems from this protest of 1529.) Faced with menacing powers on both his western and eastern frontiers, one thing that Charles did not need was a civil war. And while he temporized, hoping for a religious settlement that would make his empire whole again, the teachings of Luther spread. At the Diet of Augsburg in 1555, Charles had to accept Lutheranism as a fact of imperial life. The diet determined that the ruler of each imperial territory would decide upon the religion his state would follow. Those who did not like the religion imposed were free to leave for another state. This agreement, that recognized only the Catholic and Lutheran persuasions, was fraught with hardship and danger; but this Peace of Augsburg, as it was called, kept the empire from exploding until 1618 when new religious conflict shredded it with the 30 Years' War.

Zwingli, the Chaplain Who Hated War

Ulrich Zwingli (1484-1531), the Swiss chaplain at the battle of Marignano (he became pacifist and Protestant at the sight of that carnage), was the most popular preacher in Zurich in 1519. He protested fasting as being non-Biblical, and, in 1522, he defied the law of celibacy by marrying. Zwingli's gospel portrayed God the Father as the source of creation and of each

137

individual human act. By the Spirit, the Father saves some people to show his love, others he condemns to show his justice. The human being is not free; God is the author of every human act, sin included. Those touched by the Spirit will make an act of faith and live according to the Bible. Sinful acts will mark those chosen by God to be damned. The Mass is not a sacrifice, and any objects of art that dignify it as such are superstitious. To worship Christ in the Eucharist is worthy of a pagan because Christ is not truly present.

In 1523 Zurich's mayor and town council commanded all priests to preach Zwingli's gospel. In 1524 they stripped the churches of their altars and purged them of all artistic decoration, music included. Since the Eucharist, à la Zwingli, was nothing more than a reminder of Christ's life and death, it was not necessary to celebrate it each Sunday. Henceforward, church services were devoted to preaching the Word.

Zwingli's preachers soon converted the town councils of Berne and Basel, not to mention the ancient monastic domain of St. Gall. In general, the middle-class, no-nonsense, urban Swiss favored Zwingli, while the country forest areas remained Roman Catholic. The Catholics armed against Ulrich, and, when the Zurich reformer could not reach agreement with Martin Luther over Christ's real presence in the Eucharist (and, thereby, lost the effective military alliance of German Protestant princes), the Protestant pacifist was killed in the defense of his gospel at the battle of Kappel in 1531. His heritage to Switzerland was a grievous religious wound that not even 4 centuries of time have totally healed.

The Meaux Reformers and Martin Luther

When William Briçonnet (1472-1534), whose father had been a cardinal and protege' of Pope Leo X, became bishop of Meaux in 1516, a group of intellectuals known as the Meaux reformers received an influential protector. Led by Lefevre d'Etaple, a priest committed to Church reform, these erudite gentlemen favored a return to the Bible in sermonizing and encouraged the reading of the Bible by making a sound translation available to French Catholics. As early as 1519 a number of Luther's reforming writings came into their hands in French translation. Briçonnet and d'Etaple remained Roman Catholic, while not ceasing to advocate intellectual and spiritual reform. Others among the Meaux reformers, for example, William Farel (1489-1565) and Louis de Berquin (1490-1520) — Louis was

Luther's French translator and was burned at the stake as a heretic — saw Martin Luther as the Church's great white hope.

King Francis I, ever anxious to steal the march on his inveterate enemy, Charles V (and Pope Clement VII, still smarting from Charles' invasion of Rome in 1527, aided and abetted the French king's ambitions), winked at Lutheranism in France. He hoped, by tolerance and discussion, to win over German Protestants and thus bring peace to the empire, something Charles had failed to do. But Francis was no more successful than Charles. When, in 1534, the French Protestants, no longer content with the easygoing Francis, attacked the Mass, the French throne responded with heavy reprisals; and the day of discussions with Lutherans came to a halt.

Toward the middle 1520's William Farel deserted France to find a religiously more congenial atmosphere in Switzerland. He converted Neuchâtel to Luther's gospel and volunteered his services to the townfolk of Geneva, who were at war with their overlord, the king of Savoy, and with their Roman Catholic bishop, Peter de la Baume. Their aim was to bring Geneva into league with the Protestant Swiss cities of Berne and Zurich.

Calvin Comes to Geneva

It was in 1536 that another Frenchman named John Calvin (1509-1564) passed through Geneva en route to Strassburg from Ferrara. Calvin, a lawyer, came from a family of lawyers with an anticlerical bent. But his passion was theology and the reform of the Church. Because of his penchant for Luther, Calvin was "on the run." William Farel persuaded his compatriot to help reform the Church in Geneva. After a false start that ended in the exile of both Farel and Calvin from the city, Geneva recalled the French lawyer-turned-theologian in 1541, and Protestantism found an organizational genius to reinforce the disciplinary lags in Lutheranism.

Calvin taught that God is the Creator, and humanity's first duty is gratitude. This gratitude is expressed by becoming one with Christ in confident faith. It is the Holy Spirit who introduces a human being to Christ and "elects" him for salvation. Faith is nurtured by the preaching of the Word.

Calvin's theology is clearly delineated in *The Institutes of the Christian Religion* (translated into French by Calvin in 1541). John Calvin had no wish to consecrate the state as pope. Pastors, doctors, elders, and deacons (members of the elect who made up Calvin's Church), not secular politicians, kept law and order within the Church and established the tone of the Christian community. Calvin established the Academy of Geneva where the doctors, himself first and foremost, trained zealous ministers of the Word. These ardent ministers, in their turn, carried the "new learning" of John Calvin and his reformed Church into France, where they commanded a vast following. Meanwhile, John Knox (c. 1513-72) captured Scotland for Calvin and fathered a democratizing trend in British history.

Luther in a Cold Climate

Anticolonialism brought Lutheranism to Sweden in 1527. Gustavus Vasa (1496-1560), allied with Lutherans of the northern German trade cities, seized the government from its Danish overlord, Christian II (embarrassingly allied with the Papal States), to the rejoicing of countless Swedish nationalists. The new king seized Church property to support his regime and invited Wittenberg-educated pastors to carry out Luther's reform.

In Denmark a palace revolution toppled Christian II from his throne, where his successor, Frederick I (1523-33), set up a national Church practically independent of Rome. After an interval of civil disturbance, Christian III (1534-59) seized the throne and had John Bugenhagen (1485-1558), a Wittenberg disciple of Luther, crown him and set up a Lutheran Church for the kingdom.

Danish colonialism imposed Lutheranism upon Norway. Though the Norwegian nobility were not notably devoted to the Holy See, they did resist Lutheranism which they saw as a Danish ploy to conquer and hold Norway. Though there were German Lutheran preachers in Bergen as early as 1528, a Norwegian Lutheran Church only came to be in the year 1607.

The Calvinistic Commoners
Who Crushed Church and Crown

Henry VIII (reigned 1509-47), once a loyal ally of the Papal States in their conflict with the empire, deserted Roman Catholicism in 1534 because Pope Clement VII refused to divorce him from Katherine of Aragon, Charles V's aunt. Henry made himself supreme head of the Church of England and few refused to acknowledge his authority. The English Church, while always in communion with Rome, had also always enjoyed a certain practical independence since the days of William the Conqueror. But sympathy for the English Queen Katherine ran high, and,

140

when Henry confiscated the English monasteries to fill the pockets of the landed gentry, there was a certain amount of popular opposition that had to be put down by force. Real Lutheranism appeared upon the scene during the reign of Henry's sickly son, Edward VI (1547-53), but it was rigorously stifled once Mary Tudor (1533-58) gained the throne. Elizabeth I (1558-1603) demanded conformity to the Church of England of which she, like her father, was head. She persecuted both Roman Catholics and would-be Lutherans (and Calvinists) with regal impartiality. During her long reign Roman Catholicism succumbed, but the tone of English religion became increasingly Calvinistic. Sober, middle-class commoners in Elizabeth's parliaments were the undoing of the Catholic Mary Stuart. They were to fashion the scaffold for Charles I, and their leveling, middle-class values shaped the French Revolution.

Discussion Questions

1. With so many people interested in reforming Christ's fragile fellowship, how was it possible to tell the orthodox from the heretical?

2. How did replacing the pope with political leaders affect the fragile fellowship?

3. Compare private interpretation of the Bible with what Sebastian Franck called Luther's "paper papacy."

4. After appropriate study, discuss the backgrounds of the leading 16th-century reformers. How did their backgrounds influence their attitudes toward the Roman Catholic Church?

5. What role did nationalism play in the revolt against the Roman Catholic Church?

Chapter 15
The Middle-class Religion of Common Sense and the Revival of Paganism

———————— Some of Christ's Fragile Fellowship ————————

Reginald Pole (1500-1558) — openminded cardinal caught in the web of Pope Paul IV's politics.

Girolamo Seripando (1492-1563) — one bishop to one see, by God.

Galilei Galileo (1564-1642) — everything's new under the sun.

Matteo Ricci (1552-1610) — communicating Christianity in Chinese.

Alphonsus Liguori (1696-1787) — the warmth of God in a cold, cold world.

With the empire divided between Catholics and Protestants, the face of France pitted with Calvinist enclaves, central Europe a battleground for religious allegiance, and Scandinavia, Scotland, and England bulwarks of Protestantism, what Christendom badly needed was a general council.

But the Catholic Hapsburg emperors were reluctant, fearing religious decisions that their Lutheran subjects might fight to the death. German Protestants distrusted a papacy that might end all discussion on the faggots of the Inquisition. The French kings, delighted at the empire's disunity, never abandoned political ambitions in Hapsburg Spain and Northern Italy. The popes feared that a general council risked a renewed attack upon papal power. The lessons of the rebelling Fathers at Constance and, especially, at Florence had not been lost upon the Holy See.

Nonetheless, Pope Paul III (1534-49), with little or no cooperation from France and the Hapsburg Holy Roman Empire, convoked a general council that opened at Trent on December 13, 1545. The Council of Trent — often interrupted by plague, war, and the fanatical one-man purging of Pope Paul IV and the Inquisition (1555-59) — remained in session until December 4,

1563. Its long and checkered history clarified the faith and toughened the sinews of a Church enduring siege.

The popes, not without resistance, controlled the council's sessions by making their own people (papal legates) its chairmen. Protestants were not welcome — in fact, remembering John Hus' fate at Constance, they were not anxious to come! The spirit of Trent was not to settle totally every theological issue in the Church, but to lay down a minimal standard of doctrine that a Roman Catholic must believe. It was hoped that this could be done without alienating various schools of philosophy, perhaps at odds with each other — the Dominican Thomists and the Franciscan Scotists, for example. Therefore, formulae from the Bible were used as often as possible rather than philosophical maxims that might favor one school over another.

Decision at Trent

After long and often violent debate, the council agreed that the Bible and tradition (what the Church taught over the ages) were common sources of faith. Man is not totally corrupt, but he is freely saved by God through faith and through a grace that internally changes him. Human beings have a free will, but the council did not consider how God predestines man for glory or damnation while respecting his freedom.

The sacraments, which the council named specifically, are communicators of God's saving grace to Christians. The Mass is truly a sacrifice (the making present of Calvary for those born too late to have been there in person); and the substance of bread and wine is changed into the substance of Christ's body and blood. (This process is best described by the word transubstantiation, contrary to Luther's belief that Christ was truly present *with* the bread and wine). The language of worship is to be Latin. But the council nowhere condemned the theoretical use of the vernacular. Penance and Extreme Unction are truly sacraments, and the council established the conditions of valid Matrimony between Catholics. (It did not recognize the validity of Protestant marriages, a source of strong resentment and confusion that had to be rectified in the years ahead.)

By defending the sacraments, the Council of Trent stood foursquare behind the clerical order. Baptized Christians have not all been endowed with the same spiritual power, as Luther had claimed. Holy Orders confers a special character upon a priest. In an effort to correct clerical abuses, the council de-

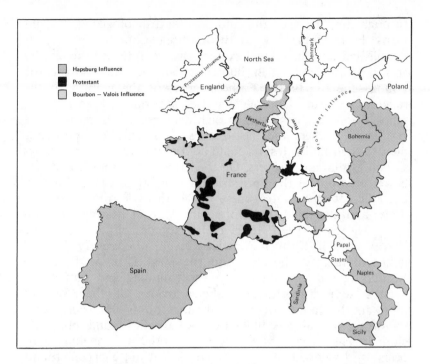

manded that bishops reside in their sees most of the year (therefore, one bishop to one see) and that seminaries be established for the spiritual and intellectual formation of the clergy. An ordained priest could not validly marry, and celibacy — in opposition to Luther, Zwingli, and Calvin — was stoutly reaffirmed.

Sage as the council's deliberations may have been, they could not reform the Church so long as they remained merely on paper. But willing men to put them into operation were not wanting.

The Soldiers of Trent

In 1544, Pope Paul III had approved, as a religious organization, a company of men led by a Spanish war veteran, Ignatius Loyola, that called themselves the Society of Jesus. (The Latin word for "society" had military overtones in the 16th century.) Vowing themselves to unswerving obedience to the popes, the Jesuits carried Trent's reforms into almost every corner of Christendom and into the Western Hemisphere and the Orient. St. Francis Xavier baptized thousands in India and planted the Church in Japan. St. Peter Canisius and St. Robert Bellarmine,

145

through simple catechizing and profound theologizing, brought many Protestants back to the Catholic Church. The Jesuits established an educational system that "baptized" the classics and developed Christian humanists among their aristocratic young scholars. In the Catholic areas of the empire, in the religious no man's land of Poland, in sect-ridden France, Jesuit schools and teachers were in high demand. The success of the Jesuits as teachers and missionaries attracted high-type young men to their ranks. Jesuits could be found in the courts of kings as confessors and advisers. On the other hand, they could also be ferreted out of the "priest holes" (hiding places) of English-Catholic country estates where Elizabeth's government hanged, drew, and quartered them for saying Mass or hearing a confession. The Society of Jesus built churches all over Catholic Europe, and in Spanish America as well, where every line and light emphasized the altar and the Mass as a sacrifice. The Jesuits figured prominently in the founding and running of Trent's seminary program. Shock troops of the Church's renewal, the Jesuits were also darlings of the Hapsburgs and, therefore, not always liked by all Catholics, some popes included. The order's very success aroused the envious and, perhaps, developed an esprit de corps that not everyone found congenial. This would lead to its eventual destruction at the hands of the Bourbon kings of Europe, beginning in 1759, until the papacy suppressed it as a religious order in 1773. In so doing, the popes lost the best friends they had ever had.

And there were others, non-Jesuits who helped the Church rise from the ashes of the Great Western Schism and the ruins of Luther's Reformation. St. Charles Borromeo, cardinal by the grace of his uncle, Pius IV (reigned 1559-65), shaped up the Church in Milan and Northern Italy by making liberal use of the Jesuits, seminaries, and the Inquisition. On the other hand, the humble St. Philip Neri, a popular parish priest of Rome, strengthened the faith of his people by his own sanctity and founded the Oratory to educate priests in the sublimity of their vocation. Ironically enough, the Oratory in France, at least, would often find itself at odds with the Jesuits in competing for seminarians. St. Francis de Sales became the teacher of everyday spirituality and made the Catholic religion fashionable in France in the 16th and 17th centuries. And the followers of St. Vincent de Paul buoyed up faltering faith in France by preaching in parishes and by training worthy priests in their seminaries (new competition for the Jesuits).

146

Politics Cloaked in Religion

The 16th century was the age of discovery, and the Spanish Hapsburgs led the pack to the New World. Just as there was a university in Spanish Mexico before Harvard ever graced Cambridge, there was also a Catholic St. Rose of Lima (Peru) long before there was a Protestant William Penn or a Jonathan Edwards. To a great extent, Catholic colonization in the Western Hemisphere (Mexico, South America, Canada, and the Mississippi Valley) compensated the Roman Catholic Church for losses in Northern Europe.

But, for all this revitalizing of the Roman Catholic Church, Christendom lay divided and polarized, Protestant against Catholic. The bitterness of the struggle between the persuasions, as well as not so pious infighting within the Church itself, fostered disgust and disbelief in formal religion. The end result of the complex and confusing political and religious events of 16th and 17th-century Western Europe was the rebirth of paganism.

The so-called Peace of Augsburg (1555) which decreed that each prince of the empire should establish and rule the Church of his choice within his domain (any disagreeing subjects being free to leave his domain, thereby forfeiting their property for their faith) settled nothing. Human beings are fickle and some German princes changed faith once, even twice, in a lifetime — with consequent dislocation of dissident subjects. These ingredients of chaos exploded in the soup called the 30 Years' War (1618-48) that scalded Western Europe. Bohemia, like Poland before it, was a no man's land of varying religious persuasions and enjoyed, like Poland, a great measure of religious toleration. When Bohemian Protestants, in 1617, demanded greater freedoms, the emperor, Ferdinand II (reigned 1619-37), who had been king of Bohemia, refused, and it was war. Allied with other Catholic princes, Ferdinand put down the Protestants in 1628.

France suffered civil war during most of the second half of the 16th century. Religious conflict occasioned it and, perhaps, canonized it; but, fundamentally, France's "religious" wars were nothing new. Catherine de Medici, widow of Henry II, was left with two young and incompetent sons to defend against more powerful and jealous counsins — the family of Guise (Catholics) and the family of Condé (Protestants) — each of whom wanted king and crown for themselves. Catherine, often opting for religious toleration, played one family against the other to save the crown, so once again it was the old battle for supremacy in France between crown and nobles. In 1572, Protestant pressures to push France into a war against Hapsburg Spain, in behalf of Calvinist rebels seeking independence in the Low Countries (ruled by Spain), proved too much for Catherine's delicate balancing act; and she eliminated the pressure by authorizing the Saint Bartholomew's Day Massacre of her not so loyal Protestant opposition. Though this bloody action diminished Protestant power within France, the Protestant Henry IV (Bourbon) came to the throne when his brother-in-law, King Henry III (Valois), was assassinated in 1589. Henry IV became a Catholic in 1593 and, in 1598, issued the edict of Nantes giving considerable religious and political freedom to French Protestants.

Richelieu's Double Religious Standard

The wily Florentine regent, Catherine de Medici, had refused to aid rebellious Protestant subjects in the Low Countries against the Spanish Hapsburgs. But the new regime — Louis XIII (Henry IV's son) and his mentor, Cardinal Richelieu (1585-1642) — considered it a strategy of state to aid and abet any Protestants abroad who would weaken the house of Hapsburg in the empire. (With Hapsburgs in Spain, Southern Italy, the Holy Roman Empire, and influential in Northern Italy, the French felt surrounded.) Richelieu, who militarily repressed Protestant political power at home, wanted the left bank of the Rhine and the Low Countries (largely Hapsburg property), if possible, securely in French hands, so he was more than willing to use Danish, Swedish, or German Protestants against the Catholic Hapsburgs. When, in 1626, the Danish-Lutheran king, Christian V, invaded the empire to get the bishopric of Osnabrück for his son, Richelieu's pocketbook paid the bill. The Austrian Hapsburg, Ferdinand II, defeated the Danish Christian V. To safeguard lines of communication between the Spanish Hapsburgs in Italy and their rebellious subjects in the Low Countries, Ferdinand's forces occupied Mantua, the key to the lower Rhine and a build-up stage for Spanish troops en route to the Netherlands.

This movement aroused all the old papal fears of Hapsburgs to the north and south of the Papal States. (Pope Urban VIII claimed that he had killed all the birds in his garden so he could sleep during the day because he could not sleep at night.) And when a Lutheran-Swedish challenger, Gustavus Adolphus

(1594-1632), invaded the empire in 1630, even the papacy seemed to become religiouly indifferent so long as the Catholic Hapsburgs were humbled. The Jesuits, Hapsburg favorites, fell from Urban's favor, and the pope was not disappointed to see Richelieu's France cross swords with the Holy Roman Empire. Finally, in 1648 — both sides utterly exhausted with France still holding strong points along the Rhine — the Bourbons and the Hapsburgs concluded the Peace of Westphalia. Once again, each prince in the empire became the "pope" of his domain — with power to determine what religion his subjects would believe! For all its desire to humiliate the Hapsburgs, the papacy witnessed the Church's loss of 2 archbishoprics, 14 bishoprics, 6 abbeys, and saw Bremen and Magdeburg become permanently Protestant, thanks to a Roman Catholic cardinal who controlled the foreign policy and treasury of France.

The Splintering of Christianity

Despite the efforts of Pietists in Germany and Methodists in England to fan the flame of the Spirit in coldly sterile state Churches, these official bodies remained largely lifeless. These evangelical endeavors only added their contribution to the splintering of Christianity: Protestant state Churches in the empire and in England that demanded conformity were no more congenial to many of their worshipers than the old Roman Catholic Church had been. Protestantism proliferated as more dissenters (our Puritan forefathers among them) fell away.

On the Iberian Peninsula and in Italy, the Spanish and Roman Inquisitions effectively kept Catholics in line: stalwart St. Ignatius Loyola and loyal St. Teresa of Avila were not above Inquisitorial suspicion, and Galileo succumbed to its threats, tragically digging a ditch between religion and science. But these methods only aroused resentment and discontent that exploded in the 19th and 20th centuries.

In France, where the Bourbon monarchs (Louis XIII, XIV, XV, and XVI, reigning 1610-1792) insisted upon one king, one faith (Catholic), one God for all Frenchmen and enforced this maxim with censorship and police action, non-Catholics squirmed at the tightening of political screws. There were always nobles at hand to use Protestant discontentment to foment civil war against the crown. Quite a number of noblemen and middle-class professional people, often less than enthusiastic about autocratic Bourbon rule, sympathized in varying degrees with a dissident Catholic group called Jansenists. (These followers of a dour Dutch theologian named Jansenius resembled the Calvinists in their sober, even harsh, outlook on religion.) The Jansenists, who emphasized the stark seriousness of religion and the utter transcendence of God, hated the Jesuits whose religious outlook was far more optimistic and humanistic. They accused the Jesuits of religious laxity and worldly ambition. Jesuit confessors to notably lax Bourbon kings seemed to embody the image. French bishops, far from being the lackeys of the kings, wanted a French Church that was largely independent of the pope while still acknowledging papal primacy of sorts. While not at all sympathetic to the Jansenists, many of the bishops distrusted religious orders with headquarters in the Papal States, particularly the Jesuits. Since most (by 1789, all) of the bishops came from the nobility, there was a great social gulf between themselves and their priests largely recruited from the peasantry. Seventeenth and eighteenth-century France produced saints — Francis de Sales, Jane Frances de Chantal, Vincent de Paul — loyally devoted to the Roman Catholic Church. But she also produced religious controversialists — Arnauld and Pascal against the Jesuits, Bossuet and Fenelon against each other — who sniped merrily, wittily, bitingly at their coreligionists to the high good humor of men who had decreed a pox on both camps and had decided to believe in nothing. All the controversy about state-sanctioned Catholicism made the Church appear to be hypocritically ridiculous — embraced as it was by a government that used religion as a means of territorial expansion abroad and repression at home. At least, so it seemed to the intellectual fathers of the French Revolution, *les philosophes.*

Religious Common Sense and Paganism

For a new religion made the scene, the religion of science and common sense. Through the nominalists of the Middle Ages to middle-class John Locke the Englishman (1632-1704), it became more and more fashionable to declare that all a man knows is what he can see, smell, touch, and measure. Spiritual truths were beyond the mind's capacity. In England, where there was a penchant for physical science and no Inquisition, Isaac Newton (1642-1727) had ceased to believe in the personal God of the Bible, and David Hume (1711-76), denying miracles, discounted the New Testament.

A French political exile in London, Francois Marie Arouet,

Voltaire (1694-1778), was a willing convert to this middle-class religion of common sense. Violently anti-Christian, he devoted his literary skills to crushing "the infamous thing," the Church, that he saw as a blight upon civilization. Denis Diderot (1713-84) dipped deeply into the writings of the English philosophers and emerged a total atheist. His efforts, coupled with the genius of Jean Le Rond d'Alembert (1717-83), produced *L'Encyclopedie,* a multivolumed encyclopedia of human knowledge inspired by down-to-earth, middle-class common sense and a militant, if discreet, hatred of Christianity which it wrote off as myth and superstition. The Swiss paranoid, Jean Jacques Rousseau (1712-78), in his masterpieces, *La Nouvelle Heloise, Emile,* and *The Social Contract,* developed a system of brainwashing citizens so that they could be formed to live in "people's republics" not unlike those of Nazi Germany or Communist China. His ambiguous and sentimental democratic vocabulary limned the slogans of the French Revolution. But his real ideal of democracy was best portrayed by Robespierre's Republic of Virtue and its inexorable Reign of Terror.

Though many of the reforms advocated by the 16th-century reformers were needed by the Church, the exploding of Christianity into warring, sectarian splinters was not. To replace this religious chaos, the religion of common sense was born. The enlightened philosophers of 18th-century France were its midwives.

In *les philosophes'* revolution of 1789, down-to-earth, no-nonsense, middle-class people, like those who had struck out at the feudal Church of the 16th century, unleashed an attack upon outmoded feudal, noble, and monarchical authority and tumbled it. In the revolutionary armies of Napoleon, people power, or the semblance of people power, reminiscent of Rousseau's dictatorial democracy, dominated Western Europe. In its middle-class aspirations for liberty, equality, and fraternity as against feudal privilege, the leveling religion of common sense undermined the other worldly aspects of Christian revelation and revived down-to-earth paganism.

Discussion Questions

1. In what ways could Trent be considered a "liberal" ecumenical council?

2. Why did Trent so strongly emphasize the sacrificial aspects of the Mass? What aspects of the Mass are emphasized today? Why?

3. Discuss the mission of the Jesuits in reforming Christ's fragile fellowship.

4. How did cloaking politics with the mantle of religion lead to practical agnosticism in the West?

5. Discuss the Galileo case and the rupture between religion and natural science. Are there any indications of the gap between religion and natural science being narrowed?

Chapter 16
The Popes' Hard-nosed Approach to the New Paganism

Some of Christ's Fragile Fellowship

Elizabeth Bayley Seton (1774-1821) — the WASP who became a saint.

Bernadette Soubirous (1844-1879) — to be poor and Catholic and see visions of the Virgin.

Antonio Rosmini-Serbati (1797-1855) — to be Italian and Catholic and be caught in-between.

Vincenzo Gioberti (1801-1852) — a united Italy under the pope and exile.

Giacomo Antonelli (1806-1876) — "Red Pope" and *eminence grise* of Pius IX.

The 19th century drew the drapes upon the age of faith. The Church, as at her beginning, confronted an exploding population of nonbelievers. Her message of otherworldly hope had less and less meaning for people preoccupied with survival in this fascinating world. For, in this century and continuing to now, the things of this world have closed in, isolating man in time and space, curtaining his quest for immortality. Down-to-earth, scientific worldliness challenges the otherworldly Good News of redemption and has often had Christianity on the ropes.

In the 19th century, three revolutions erupted in Western Europe to change human attitudes toward life. In 1789, the tidal wave of social and political revolution, brewing since Luther's 16th-century, middle-class Reformation, crested to sweep before it the outmoded feudal structure of nobility and kings. In Catholic France, where bishoprics were the preserve of the aristocracy, the Church fell with the old regime.

Accompanying the French Revolution's tide of democracy was the industrial revolution that turned man from tranquilly tilling the fields to frenetically toiling in factories to create utensils for properly coping with this world's challenges.

Lastly was the scientific revolution — beginning with Newton and Darwin and running through Freud and Einstein — that promised, and continues to do so, a mastery of this universe that will render God and his heaven irrelevant.

Each revolution threw down its gauntlet before the Catholic Church, that representative of God and his heaven, and challenged its reason for existing. The Catholic Church story, from 1789 to the present, has been the history of that duel.

The Church, Captive of the Revolution

Bankrupt in 1789, Louis XVI of France called the Estates General (representatives of the clergy, the nobility, and the common people) to straighten out the mess. The priests — separating themselves from their bishops (all of whom were nobles) and the nobility — voted, for the first time, with their own kind, commoners, for a constitution whereby the king would rule France by people-given law. In an orgy of self-sacrifice the nobles and noble bishops foresook their titles and tax-free privileges to become common citizens. The Civil Constitution of the Clergy created a state Church in France, separated from Rome, much like the Church of England. Those who did not want to join it went underground, into exile, or literally lost their heads on the guillotine.

When the armies of Austria unsuccessfully attempted to rescue Louis XVI and his wife, Marie Antoinette (the sister of Leopold II of Austria), Frenchmen sensed plotters against their revolution everywhere. Robespierre set up his Spartan Republic of Virtue, a totalitarian "people's republic" *à la* Rousseau; and the guillotine destroyed any opposition — among its victims the king and queen of France. For a brief period, pagan worship of the goddess of liberty (portrayed by an actress) replaced the Mass at Notre Dame. Inflation and depressed salaries brought Robespierre, however, to his rendezvous with the guillotine in 1794. Nevertheless, even more conservative revolutionary regimes continued to flirt with paganism until the turn of the century.

Despite the fall of Robespierre, the revolution flourished. Under the Directory the conscript armies of France invaded the Italian Peninsula — the Papal States included — and set up satellite republics and kingdoms dedicated to the "liberty, equality, and fraternity" of the French Revolution. In 1801, Napoleon, as first consul of France, signed a concordat (an

154

agreement) with Pope Pius VII (reigned 1800-23) recognizing the Roman Catholic Church as the Church of the majority of the French people. But, for all practical purposes, Napoleon, soon to become emperor of the French, kept that Church under his thumb. The pope, deprived of his Papal States, was really his prisoner at Fontainebleau.

For all his imperial trappings (and Napoleon became every inch an emperor of Charlemagneian stature), Napoleon spread broadcast the democratizing ideals of the French Revolution. To the Holy Roman Empire — which he split into the Confederation of the Rhine, Bavaria, Prussia, Austria, et al. — as well as to the Italian and Iberian Peninsulas, Napoleon brought law and order, efficient administration, respect for education and hygiene, and, at least, lip service to the ideals of liberty. His empire, constantly at war with England and varying continental challengers, was costly to maintain, and all his satellite countries were at the disposal of *la belle France* when all was said and done.

When Napoleon met his Waterloo, there were few outside of France who wept over his downfall. But middle-class Spaniards, Italians, Germans — mostly professional people in law, education, government, medicine, even religion — did not forget the ideals of liberty, equality, and fraternity. With Napoleon's battalions gone, they longed to found their own governments along the pattern of republican France. Unfortunately for Christianity, many of these middle-class aspirants to liberty also hated the Church as a medieval relic that symbolized oppression and superstition. These liberals, as they were called, usually enacted legislation calculated to destroy Christianity wherever they succeeded to power; and they did it for the sake of "progress, liberalism, and modern civilization." They had read their Voltaire, *L'Encyclopedie* and Rouseau well!

The Legacy of Liberty

After they had defeated Napoleon, the monarchical powers of Europe — the big four being England, Prussia, Austria, and Russia — restored the French throne to the heir of the Bourbon king, Louis XVIII (reigned 1814-24). Louis, whose brother, Louis XVI, had perished on the scaffold during the Reign of Terror, acted as though there had been no revolution. He returned to the Bourbon style of repressive rule. Restoring the Catholic Church to a favored position in the realm, he dubbed it the guardian of public morality. Liberals as well as Catholics resented the repressive Bourbon regime and toppled it in 1830.

In the forefront of French Catholics who were tired of monarchical tyranny was Félicité de Lamennais (1782-1854). Lamennais, a fallen-away Catholic, had returned to the Church of his Baptism when he was 22 and received Holy Orders in 1816. His *Essay on Religious Indifference* (1818) converted many irreligious Frenchmen to the Catholic Church — to the embarrassment of many Roman Catholic theologians who found much of its philosophy questionable. Lamennais resented the pious police state of the restored Bourbons and his Church in the role of scapegoat for the tyranny of Louis XVIII and his brother, Charles X (reigned 1824-30). In his newspaper, *L'Avenir* (The Future), Lamennais thumped for the complete separation of Church and state. The future belonged to democracy, said Lamennais. The Church, caught in kingly embrace, would fall when the people eventually overthrew kings for good and all.

Nor was Lamennais the only French Catholic who felt this way. Two powerful sympathizers were Henri Lacordaire (1802-61), a brilliant lawyer turned priest and preacher, and Count Charles Montalembert (1810-70), the champion of free Catholic schools in France. In 1863, at the Congress of Malines (Belgium), the count, who had devoted his life and fortune to keeping the French government out of Catholic schools, called also for complete separation of Church and state. What was needed was a "free Church in a free state," much as existed in Belgium and the United States.

In Germany, John Joseph Döllinger (1799-1890), long-time battler with the Lutheran-Prussian kings who had tried to stifle Catholicism in their domains, pleaded for academic freedom for German-Catholic scientists who felt themselves hampered by the Church's censorship and Rome's emphasis on the almost exclusive use of Thomistic philosophy in theological research. Being a historian, Döllinger wanted greater use of historical and linguistic sciences in searching the Scriptures.

In England, the illustrious scholar-convert, John Henry Newman (1801-1890), joined the cause of democracy as early as 1859 by publishing an article called, "On Consulting the Faithful on Matters of Doctrine" (*Rambler*, July 1859).

The Popes as Chaplains of the Holy Alliance

The papacy's response to the surge of Catholic democracy

was predictable — even understandable.

Since the 4th century, the Church had been the official religion teacher of the Roman Empire. When that empire had collapsed in the West before barbarian hordes, it had been the Church that had civilized these near savages in the spirit of Christ and Rome. It, with a handful of strong men (kings and nobles), had shaped law and order out of chaos. Commissioned by Christ, the Church, with the popes in the lead, had been accustomed to being heard and obeyed. Since the 16th century the pope's Church had had to deal with malcontent, middle-class rebels, and their revolt had cost civilization dearly. In successfully striking out against ecclesiastical authority, the natural consequence of their rebellion had culminated in the disaster of 1789 — the overthrow of the state and the restoration of paganism.

But now, thanks to a Holy Alliance of European kings (so felt the popes), that revolt was at an end. Christian civilization

The political situation in Italy as it might have been pictured by an editorial cartoonist of the times.

would be restored with the Roman Catholic Church as its bastion. The Protestant king of England, the Orthodox czar of Russia, and the Catholic emperor of Austria had seen this as the Church's mission and had, therefore, restored Pope Pius VII and his successors to the Papal States once they had finished with Napoleon. The papacy was embarrassed with Catholic believers in Poland and Ireland who wanted to disturb this restoration of civilization (as the popes saw it) by uprisings against Russia and England in the name of liberty. In the Italian Peninsula itself were liberals who wanted a united Italy. Prodded on by men who hated the Church — such as the kings of Piedmont-Savoy (Charles Albert and Victor Emmanuel) and the partisan, Garibaldi — Italian liberals had risen against their Austrian overlords in the North and against the king of Sicily in the South. And they plotted rebellion in the Papal States themselves, threatening to dethrone the popes and set up a united Italian kingdom.

Should that happen, thought the popes, the Church would fall and, with it, all Christian civilization. The Church, aided by the state, must be free to accomplish Christ's mission of spreading the Good News; and that freedom depended upon the integrity of responsible royal rule and the independence of the Papal States — an independence for which so much blood had been shed throughout the Middle Ages. Those who destroyed kings in the name of freedom and those who wanted a united Italy at the expense of the Papal States were the enemies of Christian civilization, so the popes felt. The political structure of king and Christian Church ruling over a largely illiterate peasantry — never mind the snappish malcontents of the middle class — was the only civilization that popes like Pius VII Leo XII, Pius VIII, Gregory XVI, or Pius IX (reigning 1846-78) had ever known. Godless democrats demanding power to strike down Church and king for the sake of "progress, liberalism, and modern civilization" meant nothing but the restoration of paganism. Therefore, the pope's answer to liberals, even so-called Catholic liberals, was, "No!"

The "No-No" of Catholic Liberalism

In 1834, Gregory XVI (1831-46) condemned the liberal teaching of Félicité de Lamennais and the Frenchman left the Church. Rome forced Newman to give up the *Rambler* after reading his democratic suggestion to consult the faithful on matters of doctrine. Whenever Pius IX (1846-78) heard talk of a "free Church in a free state," such as that of Montalembert at Malines, it could only remind him of the anticlerical, Italian liberal, Camillo Cavour (1810-1861). As premier of the king of Piedmont, Cavour had confiscated Church property, had taken over the Papal States (except the city of Rome), after plebiscites that registered surprisingly little resistence, and formed a united Italy under Victor Emmanuel II (reigned 1861-78) — all in the name of a "free Church in a free state." In March 1864, the pope warned Montalembert that, Catholic champion or not, he was sailing fearfully close to the wind. Döllinger, who was just a little bit smug about his Teutonic learning, had pointed out in his book, *The Papacy and Temporal Power*, that there was no essential connection between the independent possession of the Papal States and papal primacy; he had suggested, rather superciliously, that the Italian Pius IX ought to leave his states to Piedmont and seek refuge in Germany where he could complete his education. But the pope warned him to toe the mark of the Church's guidelines, particularly in the use of scholastic philosophy as a handmaid to theological research. Pius wanted no more adventure in theology than he wanted in politics! He unfortunately widened the gap between science and religion.

The Industrial Revolution Rip Off

The harnessing of steam power for the use of industry had the result of concentrating more and more wealth in the hands of fewer and fewer people. The new machines of industry were expensive to buy and maintain. They successfully competed with handcrafted goods — cloth, for example — driving small industries out of business. They reduced the need of hired hands on the farm, and cities that had factories swelled with people seeking work. This proletariat was at the mercy of a handful of machine owners who let the economic law of supply and demand determine the livelihood of factory hands with nary a thought of their obligations to society. Working conditions were generally inhuman and there were few who worried about the workingman's plight. One who did was a German middle-class theorist, Karl Marx (1818-83). In his *Communist Manifesto* (1848) he called upon the workers of the world to unite and take over the machines after liquidating the owners. Marx was godless, believing that Christianity was an opiate that lulled people into accepting their sorry lot with the promise of "pie in the sky by and by." The Communist world of our day, that thrives on the economically oppressed, witnesses quite effectively to the quality of Marx' genius.

Leadership at the Top Lacking

Despite the fact that the Church was losing adherents to the cause of socialism, it was slow to offer any answers to the abuses of the industrial revolution. It understood an agricultural society, but the problems of the proletariat were puzzling. Its moral theology during most of the 19th century reckoned the relationship of workingman to boss as that of child to parent. In countries little touched by industry, such as Spain or Italy, it made small difference. In industrialized France, where most of the clergy came from farms, priests had little sympathy for factory hands and these workers abandoned their faith in droves.

In Germany, England, and the United States, where many priests came from workingmen's families, the Catholic Church acted more vigorously in the defense of proletarian rights. Churchmen encouraged the formation of workingmen's associations that could command better wages in negotiating with employers and pressured elected politicians into passing laws that protected the laborer's rights. Here the Church suffered fewer losses to socialism. But the popes, preoccupied with the march of Piedmont on the Papal States and trying to hold a largely discontented populace in line, had little leisure to devote to the downtrodden worker. In the fight for the proletariat, leadership at the top was sadly lacking throughout the first three quarters of the 19th century.

Pius IX Hard-noses Paganism

On December 8, 1864, Pope Pius IX confronted the new paganism. In his encyclical, *Quanta Cura*, to which he attached a *Syllabus Errorum* (a list of errors), the pope condemned the evolutionary theorizing of Darwin, the godless socialism of Marx, exaggerated popular sovereignty and unlimited freedom of the press — to mention only a few items under consideration. In article 80 the pope condemned the idea that " ... The sovereign pontiff ought to come to terms with progress, liberalism, and modern civilization." The "progress, liberalism, and modern civilization" Pius had in mind were camouflage concepts used by anticlerical liberals to justify their attacks on the Church. But to the average Catholic or non-Catholic man of good will it sounded as though the papacy stood foursquare against life, liberty, and the pursuit of happiness. Most people in

America or England, often indifferent to religion and little understanding the ferocity of French, Spanish, or Italian anti-clerical liberals in their hatred of the Church, thought that poor Pius had lost his mind. He seemed like the man who shouted, "Stop the world! I want to get off!" Despite Church analysts who pointed out that the pope was only condemning certain radicals who sought to destroy Christianity in the name of a new paganism that called itself liberal, the encyclical with its list of errors seemed to give truth to the charge that the Catholic Church was a dismal relic of the Dark Ages.

Then, adding insult to injury (or, at least, so it seemed to many an observer), Pope Pius IX convoked Vatican Council I on December 8, 1869. During its turbulent sessions the errors of the age (*Syllabus Errorum*) were solemnly condemned and a vast majority of the Fathers declared the pope infallible in matters of faith and morals. (A sizable minority of the Fathers of the council absented themselves when the final vote on infallibility came, not because they did not believe him infalli-ble, but because they did not think that papal infallibility was an idea whose hour had come — with the Church on the ropes, pummeled, as it were, by the fists of science, economy, and pagan anticlericalism.)

When the French troops that had been guarding Rome against the threatening power of Piedmont (Victor Emmanuel wanted Rome to be the capital of his new "Italy") were called home in 1870 to defend their country against Prussian invaders, it looked as though the infallible Pius' anticlerical enemies had the last laugh. Victor Emmanuel's army poured into the Eternal City, to the satisfaction of most Romans and the outraged humiliation of the pope. Pius, protesting that he had been robbed, locked himself in the Vatican and refused to recognize "Italy." And his gleeful enemies believed, at long last, that they had closed the book on the Catholic Church story.

Discussion Questions

1. As a result of the French Revolution compare the relation-ship of the Church with 19th-century western society and Christ's fragile fellowship in the beginning.

2. Why did the 18th-century enlightened philosophers have more influence on the shaping of democracy than the Church?

3. Why did the 19th-century popes oppose the idea of "a free Church in a free state"?

4. What legacy does Marx' classless society owe to the philosophers of the French Revolution?

5. Discuss John Henry Newman's, "On Consulting the Faithful on Matters of Doctrine."

Chapter 17
The Church in the "Brave New World"

―――――――――Some of Christ's Fragile Fellowship―――――――

Wilhelm Emmanuel von Kettler (1811-1877) — from student beer halls to social legislation.
Terence Vincent Powderly (1849-1924) — knights to defend the workingman.
Rafael Merry del Val (1865-1930) — crop and bridle of a saint.
Luigi Sturzo (1871-1957) — Catholic victim of Catholic Action?
Edith Stein (1891-1942) — Catholic victim of Catholic protest.

Because neither France nor Austria, cowed by Prussian military might, needed new enemies in the Italian Peninsula, they would not lift a finger to defend Rome from the invading Piedmontese. Disgruntled, Pius IX locked himself a "prisoner in the Vatican" and refused in any way to recognize the new Italian government. Italian Catholics, who overwhelmingly supported a united Italian nation, were told to take no active part in the new regime, for this would tend to condone the theft of the Papal States. Quite obviously the pope's Catholics did not conform to Pius' hard-nosed approach to politics on the peninsula (Rome's Catholic population voted 40,785 to 46 for annexation to the new united kingdom of Italy); but the papal prohibition stifled any organization of a Catholic political party in the new kingdom.

In the midst of the "pork-barrel" demagoguery that characterized Italian politics from the 19th century to the reign of Mussolini, a disciplined Catholic political party might have brought order out of chaos and might have deprived the future Fascists of any reason for existence. Noncooperation with the Italian kingdom simply gave the new liberal politicos the only issue they agreed upon — their common contempt for priests and religion. In the name of "prog-

Mussolini

163

ress, liberalism, and modern civilization," Italian anticlericals soon confiscated Church funds and encouraged municipalities to abolish free religion classes. The role of the priest in public life was reduced to the confines of the Church's sanctuary and sacristy. Instead of alleviating Italy's medieval poverty, most Italian politicians endorsed bootless adventures in Abyssinia and the empty glory of being the Allies' poor country cousin in World War I. Mussolini and his disciplined Black Shirts were around to pick up the pieces of a country smashed beneath the burden of inflation, bankruptcy, and hopelessness. And that was the end of progress, liberalism, and modern civilization in any sense of the words.

But if the popes did not take kindly to the despoliation of their real estate, they were inevitably relieved of the responsibility and the liability of ruling a handful of discontented Italians who had once been citizens of the Papal States. Catholics outside of Italy saw the successive "prisoners of the Vatican" as martyrs to the cause of justice, and even non-Catholics took a kindlier view of a victimized, impotent pope. Suffering enhanced the moral stature of the papacy throughout the world and rendered the popes far more conscious of their role as shepherds of all men. Men of the measure of Leo XIII, St. Pius X, and Benedict XV, not relinquishing an inch of their rights to the Papal States, saw themselves more and more as the leaders of all Catholics throughout the world; and they sought means of accommodating their Church to the changed situation "progress, liberalism, and modern civilization" had wrought in so many countries of Western Europe.

France's War on the Church

In Paris, the cold-blooded killing of Archbishop Georges Darboy during the desperate Communard rebellion of 1871 betokened the martyrdom the Church of France was to suffer over the next half-century at the hands of anticlerical, liberal governments. The Ferry Laws dissolved religious orders and stripped Catholic schools of any state aid. By 1886 only lay people were allowed to teach in schools and holding religion classes was forbidden. Catholic hospitals, asylums, even cemeteries, were confiscated. As a consequence, French-Catholic tempers flared. Catholics (many in the military), with their nonreligious French compatriots, yearned to avenge themselves upon the new German Empire for their defeat at the hands of the Prussians in "1871. Catholics (many of whom wished a restoration of the monarchy) hated the antireligious govern-ments of the French republic. Little wonder that they were shocked and outraged when Pope Leo XIII (reigned 1878-1903), in an effort to reconcile the battered French Church with the Third Republic, called upon the Catholics of France to accept their belligerent, nonbelieving government. Leo realized that the Church's mission of spreading Christ's Good News transcended any hostile government and that it could survive any regime.

Leo XIII

But Leo's attempts at peacemaking failed. By 1904, the government of Justin Combes (an ex-seminarian and a Free-mason) could boast that it had rid France of 13,904 Catholic schools. In 1905, the government cut all relations with the Holy See. In need of money, it wanted all the Church's property in France. In a dramatic gesture, another despoiled "prisoner of the Vatican," Pope St. Pius X (reigned 1903-14), surrendered every Church building in France to the anticlerical regime and resolved that the French Church would survive with honor as a totally private institution supported solely by the generosity of the French faithful. Only World War I — in which 5,800 (out of 45,000) French-Catholic priests gave their lives for the Third Republic — softened the anticler-ical stance of successive French governments that had perse-cuted the Church in the name of "progress, liberalism, and modern civilization."

Bismarck's Protestant Persecution

Bismarck

In Otto von Bismarck's new German Empire (1871), the Church suffered more at the hands of a perennial, Protestant-Prussian anti-Catholicism than at the hands of anticler-ical liberals. The Falk Laws of 1872, the May Laws of 1873-74, all the so-called Bread-basket Laws of the 1870's were militant attempts to subject the Church totally to the German state. But rising industrialization in the empire created a discontented proletariat that could easily fall prey to the propaganda of socialism. Protestant Bismarck feared pagan socialism far more than he hated the Catholic Church. Therefore, though despising them, he frequently allied himself with the politicians of the Catholic Center Party in the Reichstag. The Catholic Center was a German political party that was sensitive to the injustices the workingman suffered at the hands of 19th-century machine owners. It carried on a campaign to better the workingman's lot by law. The Center Party often found itself in alliance with Bismarck's government in putting through the most enlightened social legislation that any workingman enjoyed in Western Europe. Laws controlling working conditions, hours of labor, feminine and child labor, and unemployment compensation robbed the much-feared socialists of a cause, and kept Bismarck tranquil and the kaiser in power. All this gradually gentled the attitude of the Protestant state toward the Catholic Church. By 1885, Bismarck and Leo were so friendly that the Protestant statesman asked the Catholic pope to settle a dispute between Germany and Spain over the Caroline Islands. Pope Leo, in his turn, conferred the highest papal decoration, the Order of Christ, upon the former scourge of the Church, Otto von Bismarck. Though Leo could not accomplish reconciliation in France, he did accomplish it in Germany — mainly through diplomacy and a dynamic Catholic political party. Despite the reliance upon Catholic democratic politicians in Germany, Leo (and this was typical of almost all of the 20th-century popes) distrusted democracy in general and could find no place for Catholics in the politics of the upstart, democratic Italian kingdom. He had no intention of admitting that that government even existed!

The Popes' Response to Irresponsible Capitalism

Although Leo floundered when faced with the hostility of the French Revolution, he succeeded in Germany perhaps because he was faced with century-old Protestant opponents whom the Church was used to handling. His "German experience" with Bismarck and the Catholic Center Party equipped him and many of his successors (Pius XI, Pius XII, John XXIII, and Paul VI) to come to grips with the economic revolution. Influenced by the social and economic studies of the International Union of Fribourg (a clearing house of Catholic social thought in Western Europe), Leo XIII issued his *Rerum Novarum* (1891) as a Christian response to the evils of pagan socialism and irresponsible economic liberalism.

In his encyclical, the pope defended the right of private property, but he also pointed out the responsibilities that ownership entailed. Workingmen, at the mercy of private enterprise, had a God-given right to a living wage, not only for themselves but for the family that depended upon them. Workers could form associations and might even go on strike to defend their rights if, in a dispute over labor conditions or wages, all other avenues of mediation failed. *Rerum Novarum,* coupled with the later social encyclicals of Popes Pius XI, Pius XII, John XXIII, and Paul VI, charts out a full-blown plan for the equitable stewardship of this world's goods based upon national and international cooperation between owners, consumers, and their governments. Just as many prosperous Catholics muttered, "Socialism!" upon perusing Leo's initial effort in the economic sphere, so also today there are many people who think the popes too radical in the limitations they place upon the right to private property. Yet, when all is said and done, perhaps the papal blueprint for arbitrary international cooperation in the use of worldly goods is far safer and saner than the other option — the use of military force to assure sources of power, food, and water for the survival of the fittest.

The Modernist Overkill

In confronting the scientific revolution of the 19th century, the "prisoners of the Vatican" were far less venturesome. We have seen the hard-nosed attitude of Pius IX when faced with the cries of Döllinger for academic freedom. German-Protestant theological explorers, using ancient languages and the historic method in sounding Sacred Scripture, greatly influenced their Catholic colleagues throughout Western Europe. When David F. Strauss (1808-74) mused in 1836 that Jesus was simply a legend illustrating the dialectic philosophy of Hegel, Joseph Ernest Renan (1823-92) popularized his ideas in his slightly blasphemous, but widely read, *Life of Jesus* (1863). In 1900, German Adolf Harnack published *The Essence of Christianity,* in which he denied the possibility of any knowledge of a historic Jesus.

Harnack

All man knows, said Harnack, is the kernel of an unknown Christ's message: The kingdom of God is life *lived on this earth* in the sight of God. The rest is myth. Alfred F. Loisy (1857-1940), a French Bible expert, less than candidly took up the cudgel against Harnack in 1902, when he published *The Gospel and the Church.* The more he railed against Harnack, the more his book, when analyzed, seemed to agree with the German scholar: The otherworldly Christ of popular Christian-

167

ity was actually the creation of the Church; therefore, it was nothing but a myth. The kingdom of God that the real (but unknown) Christ taught was nothing but a meaningful life on this earth.

The archbishop of Paris promptly condemned Loisy's work. But the situation did not end there. French priests and Catholics, already goaded beyond endurance by their anticlerical government, became slightly paranoid in the defense of the "old-time religion." In the face of persecution, only foursquare (the French called it *integral*) Catholics would do. Any scholar, priest or layman, who delved into theology, history, or politics with an aura of open-mindedness became suspect to these baited French-Catholics. Doubtlessly, some would-be heretics were nipped in the bud by the vigilance of France's integral Catholicism, but this vigilance took on the aspects of a witch hunt. And Rome, that had traditionally played a cool hand in the historic poker of French Church affairs, became infected with France's hysteria. In 1907 and 1909, Pope St. Pius X condemned the conclusions of Loisy concerning Christ and the Church as a heresy called Modernism. Unfortunately, the pope not only condemned Loisy's teaching (which was unorthodox) but also, seemingly, his manner of investigation (the use of the Bible's original languages, the study of Hebrew literature, and the historic method in sounding Scripture's meaning — a thoroughly legitimate approach to Biblical interpretation). St. Pius' encyclical, *Pascendi* (1909), encouraged the investigation of seminary professors. Each diocese was to set up a censor of Church publications, sifting copy for traces of Modernism either in doctrine or research method. In 1910, Pius imposed an anti-Modernist oath upon all seminary professors and pastors of the faithful. In Italy a certain Monsignor Benigni ran a "sacred CIA" agency called *Sapinère* to ferret out of seminary faculties professors suspected of Modernism. (This agency came to light when, in 1914, Germans occupying Belgium broke the cover of *Sapinère* agents thinking that they had unearthed an Allied spy ring!)

Real as the heresy of Modernism was, this Roman reaction was the height of overkill. Loisy had never enjoyed a popular following. But this inquisitorial espionage had the effect of suppressing legitimate scholarship in the Church. For example, Monsignor Pierre Batiffol, an eminent Church historian, lost his position as rector of the Catholic Institute of Toulouse because of his historic speculations on the Eucharist. Between

1908-1913 Henri Bremond and Louis Duchesne found that some of their writings on history were prohibited to Catholics. Even the outstanding Biblical scholar, Marie Joseph Lagrange — the Dominican friar whom Pope Leo XIII had named to head the Pontifical Biblical Commission in the interests of more scientifically plumbing the Scriptures — was out of bounds to seminarians when much of his research became forbidden reading.

This sort of intimidation discouraged original approaches to theology. It may have held the line of orthodoxy but, ironically enough, it implied its own heresy: that all the mysteries of Christianity were no longer mysteries but perfectly clear, and that there was no longer any need of the Holy Spirit's enlightenment nor the desirability of the probing light of human thought to deepen the maturity of Catholic contemplation. As a conse-

John XXIII

quence, Catholic theological and Biblical research went into the decline of hibernation (though, all credit due him, Pope Pius XII pioneered sound paths of Biblical and theological study) until kissed into awareness by Pope John XXIII's charming open-mindedness in the early 1960's. Then, unfortunately, the so-called "new theology" exploded like a bomb, a dud dropped long ago, buried but not disarmed, lying there waiting to be detonated by some careless child at play in the long-forbidden fields of theological research. And there were as many victims of its white-hot heat as there were those illumined by its radiant light.

The Holocaust of Christian Civilization

But battles between German, French, and Italian theologians were soon to be buried beneath the mud and blood of the trenches on the Western Front. The French Revolution's ideal of democratic self-determination had proven an embarrassment to the papacy in the 19th century; for it had pitted Catholic Pole against Orthodox Russian, Catholic Irishman against Protestant Englishman, and Catholic Northern Italian against Catholic Austrian overlord. Slav minority members of the multinational Austro-Hungarian Empire grew restive and resentful under the Teutonic control of the Hapsburgs. To aid and comfort them in their cause stood the giant mother of all Slavs, Russia. When a Serbian terrorist's bullet took the life of the Hapsburg Archduke Francis Ferdinand in the Balkan town of

Sarajevo on June 28, 1914, the curtain went up on World War I. Leisure for Catholic theological controversy ceded to Catholic chauvinism, and there was little the Church could do to avert the war of nations. French Catholics yearned for revenge against Germany, and German Catholics were zealous to show how patriotic they could be in the defense of their Protestant kaiser. Pope Benedict XV (reigned 1914-22), sympathetic to Catholic Austria, bent every effort to end the 4-year senseless slaughter that had engulfed the world. His 7-point peace plan (1917), acceptable to Austria but spurned by all the other belligerents, might have ended the war; and its spirit of charity and justice might well have forestalled the ignominies of the Versailles Treaty and World War II.

The spirit of greed that Leo XIII had deplored in *Rerum Novarum* enveloped the world during the 1920's. Mussolini and his Fascists took over the Italian kingdom in 1922, due to the economic chaos that devoured the nation as the result of a war it could not afford to fight. Following a lead of Benedict XV, Pope Pius XI (reigned 1922-39) negotiated a treaty with the Italian government that acknowledged the Vatican as a sovereign state in exchange for the pope's renunciation of the Papal States. Thus, only in 1929, did the Holy See abandon the medieval principle that the ownership of land was essential to authority. Benito Mussolini, a liberal, anticlerical, religious scoffer, was also a realist. Most Italians were Catholics. If he was to carry out his Fascist reform of the Italian nation, the Church's blessing would make for good public relations both nationally and internationally. In negotiating this Lateran Treaty with Mussolini and his later concordat with Adolf Hitler

Hitler

(1933), Pius XI renounced any political role for the Church in either Fascist Italy or Nazi Germany and thereby undermined the influence of the pro-Catholic Popular Party in Italy and the Center Party in Germany. Pius XI, an autocratic individual leading an autocratic Church, frankly distrusted democracy. The chaos of the 1930's Great Depression he saw as the result of irresponsible democracy. He felt that only strong men of the stamp of Mussolini and Adolf Hitler could save the world from creeping Communism. He relied upon a grass-roots, nonpolitical organization that he had founded, Catholic Action, to permeate the world with Christ's values and save civilization. Inevitably, these irreligious dictators betrayed his hopes for a better world (and the hopes of many an American, French, and English politician who had also trusted them) by destroying the Church-led Catholic Action groups. It was then, and well before any other sovereign state, that the same autocratic Pius condemned Fascism and Nazism in his encyclicals *Non Abbiamo Bisogno* (1931) and *Mit brennender Sorge* (1937).

The human holocaust of the Nazis' World War II, with their Darwinian, "survival of the fittest" philosophy — condemned in its early stages by 19th-century Pius IX in his list of errors, *Syllabus Errorum* — and death camps simply confirmed the fact that the Church was failing to effectively communicate Christ's Good News to mankind. With peace restored, it was time for the Church to take stock of herself. Pope John XXIII convoked Vatican Council II.

Discussion Questions

1. Compare the studied hatred of Christ's fragile fellowship by French democracy with the studied indifference of American democracy.

2. Study the evolution of papal socio-economic theory from feudal obedience to the equalitarianism of Paul VI. How can one explain this evolution?

3. In a political democracy, should Christ's fragile fellowship lobby for its ideals? Why or why not?

4. Compare Pope Pius X's suppression of Modernism with the contemporary papacy's patience with theological speculation.

5. What is the relationship between Darwinian-Spencerian "survival of the fittest" philosophy, the Nazi death camps of World War II, and certain contemporary "quality of life" philosphers who would use abortion, fetal experimentation, compulsory sterilization, and euthanasia to improve the world?

Chapter 18
Facing the Future

The "brave new world" of "progress, liberalism, and modern civilization" had malfunctioned. The broken bodies and buildings of World War II witnessed all too clearly to the triumph of barbarism when the common sense *can* of science snapped the restraining leash of Christianity's *ought*. Unleavened by the Good News of Christ, "progress, liberalism, and modern civilization" had delivered the world to the forces of despair and disbelief.

Though Pope John XXIII (1958-63) urged the Fathers of Vatican Council II (1962-65) to be optimistic about the Church in this new pagan world, he could not pretend that if they were quiet it would go away. The Church's record in the face of the new world's problems was not impressive. For example, the Gospel, as communicated by the Church, had failed to temper the exaggerated demands for national liberty that had plunged the world into two global wars; for that matter, so had socialism, the new gospel of liberation, failed. The Church's strictures against economic greed (*Rerum Novarum* and *Quadragesimo Anno*), largely unacceptable even to Catholics, had not staved off the Great Depression; but neither had Marx' *Das Kapital* done so. Nor had *Mit brennender Sorge* nor the fifth commandment mitigated the horrors of Hitler's death camps — despite all the warnings in the 19th century of Pius IX against Darwin's theories on selective evolution. The unvarnished truth was that the Church was involved in a failure to communicate: It had, as in the 1st century, the Good News of Jesus Christ, but no one was buying any. The Red Cross, sadly enough, had more influence on modern society than the Catholic Church. Nor was anyone in the world more aware of this than Pope John XXIII and his brother bishops assembled in council at the Vatican in the fall of 1962.

The Church, as a second creation — the first creation gave mankind natural, limited life — through Baptism, cast mankind into the realm of godlike, unlimited life beginning on this earth and ending never. But it had become, unfortunately, something very like a club. Even many of its adherents seemed to consider it to be a kind of supernatural Rotary to which interested people *belonged.* It had its president (the pope), its officers (bishops, priests, Brothers, and nuns), its members (lay Catholics), and its sentimental loyalties (fish on Friday, ashes in Lent); but surely it was hardly the vital fiber of a new living organism. A case in point characterized this "club" attitude well. During World War II, certain Allied political leaders worried about American-Catholic reaction to a proposed bombing of Rome that might expose the pope to physical danger. Worried solely about possible Catholic sensitivity to the pope's vulnerability, never once did these men (all nominal Christians) ever trouble themselves about a Christian reaction to bombings in general — whether over Berlin, Hamburg, Hiroshima, or Nagasaki. (The attitude of Axis leaders is not to the point, since they were, self-avowedly, fine examples of the new, no-nonsense, practical, pagan world). These Christian leaders knew that there was no need to worry about a general Christian reaction, for Christianity was no longer a way of life. It was a club whose rules could be bent to getting on with the war in the most practical way possible.

Putting the Church into the Swim

Vatican Council II and its "changes in the Church" were a Holy Spirit-inspired effort to put the Church once again in the human swim. The Fathers of the council emphasized the Church's God-given role in human society as the conveyor of Christ's Good News: A loving Father has sent his Son to die and rise from the dead for humanity's sins. Faith and confidence in Christ and in what he stands for are the passports to the kingdom of God, beginning in time and enduring forever. Before God, all men and women are equal, sons and daughters (and, therefore, brothers and sisters) of a Father who cares. They are the People of God, called to reveal this Good News to all members of the human family. The Church is not their club. It is the womb of their nurturing mother, giving them life both here and hereafter.

Man exists to praise and thank God. The People of God the Father has commissioned priests. Consecrated by their Baptism into the one sacrifice that the Father wants — his Son's death and Resurrection — they renew it daily in the manner that the Son showed them at the Last Supper, the first of all Masses. The Mass is truly Christ's one sacrifice, symbolically renewed down through the ages for people born too late to be at Calvary in person. It is the daily endorsement of man's baptismal treaty that accepts God as his Father and Friend. The council taught that the Mass is a family dinner where friends meet to nourish their Christian lives with good food (the Eucharist) and good conversation (God's word in the Bible). Realization of their kinship, so the council hoped, would knit a community of believers into a Christian way of life in this world. Their lives would witness to God's vitality in all the events of their neighborhood.

Returning the Church to the People of God

Therefore, the Church, hearkening back to some of the renegade prophets of the second Reformation (Luther, Zwingli, Calvin, etc.), invited God's people to search the Scriptures more closely and reverently. To make this easier, she adopted the vernacular so that each person might hear, in his own language, what God has to say (not, as Luther held, because faith comes exclusively from hearing, and the liturgy, therefore, *must* be in the vernacular). Ironically enough, Vatican Council II took away the altars and replaced them with tables as the middle-class reformers of the 16th century had done, but not for the same reason. The reformers felt the Mass to be a hoax perpe-trated upon a baptized, priestly people by social pariahs who claimed the priesthood as their exclusive domain. Without aban-doning the special office of priesthood that is empowered to change bread and wine into Christ's body and blood, Vatican Council II reaffirmed the baptismal priesthood of Christians who offer their sacrifice, made present in the dimensions of a dinner by an agent taken from among themselves who has received the sacrament of Holy Orders. The priest's task of supplying the sacrificial table is special; but his office does not diminish the dignity of his baptized brothers and sisters. To show this, the council ordered the priest to face the people so that all, together, could present the sacrificed Mystical Body of Christ to the Father. Presentation of the bread and wine, along with the Sunday collection, characterized Mass goers as givers of God's gift. More friendly informality in attempts at folk music and the use of ordinary instruments like the guitar was an effort to encourage people to actively share in the Mass and to share with each other — this latter signified by the sign of peace.

The council, without diminishing the Christ-given authority structure in the Church (pope and bishops), encouraged the faithful to a more active role in running their communities through the formation of parish councils. Here, once again, the Church gently put into practice a lesson that the 16th-century reformers had taught with such violence: The Church is more than the pope, the bishops, the priests — it is the People of God.

Division has weakened Christianity and paganism has filled the void. Therefore, the council encouraged reconciliation with non-Catholic Christians and set an example by inviting many to sit in on its sessions. On the day before the council ended, Pope Paul expressed public regret for the excommunication of Michael Cerularius in 1054 and the succeeding events that split the Western Church from the Eastern.

To better understand the attitudes of non-Catholic Christians, it pressed for a deeper study of the Bible by all scientific means, trusting its scholars, even the most venturesome, to be men of good will and truth seekers. Such academic freedom risked the hubbub of heresy, but it also witnessed to the Church's confidence that God's Spirit had not abandoned her. Since then, teams of Catholic and Protestant scholars have studied together issues such as a common translation of the Bible, the Eucharist, and the place of the papacy in the Christian Church.

Reinforcing Self-respect

Pointing out that God is the Father of all and that non-Christian religions have truths to be revered, the Fathers of the council called for respect of the human conscience and religious freedom. Again, this was a hearkening back to the anguished cries of many 16th-century reformers. Without denying the Church's authority to inform consciences (as the 16th-century reformers, unfortunately, had done), it was a recognition of the fact that faith is inner directed, cannot be forced, and that mere external conformity is a dangerously phony facsimile. Conformity might mean that no one would rock the boat; but, should the bark become battered by wind and waves, the conformists would be the first to take to the lifeboats and abandon the ship to the deep six.

Out of reverence for conscience, the Church, in the spirit of the council, has left much of her life style up to each responsible believer. Without downgrading the need for penance, she has mitigated fast and abstinence laws, leaving individual types of self-denial up to personal choice. Underscoring the need of sorrow for sin, the practice of the sacrament of Penance is becoming more communal in its nature. For sin is not a private affair; it touches everyone in the community. So-called ecumenical marriages, respecting the non-Catholic's good faith in religious commitment, have come into vogue. It is the responsibility of the Catholic in a mixed marriage to see that the children of that marriage are raised as Catholics. Here the Church puts this responsibility squarely where it belongs.

In seeking to come to an understanding of "progress, liberalism, and modern civilization," the Church has narrowed the gap between science and religion. The findings of modern psychology, for example, have revealed as never before the complexity of the human being. Their use has given aid to a more fruitful communication of the Good News. The need of self-knowledge and self-acceptance, as a key to human maturity, is fulfilled in the Gospel message that humanity was bought at the price of God's blood. That men should accept themselves as being so loved is the only hope for the human race. And this is the content of the Church's Good News.

The Scandal of Jesus

In the Western world, Christians have become a minority group. The pagan philosophy of "You only go around once in this life . . . . " predominates. Within the next 10 years our losses may even be greater. The only people who will remain really Christian will be those who choose to be, for they will find themselves bucking the opinions of the majority. But this will be nothing new to the Catholic Church. It is the way she started. And with the help of the Spirit she will start again.

For all her human failings the Church has been the mother of Western civilization. If it is not the best of all possible civilizations, that is because this is not the best of all possible worlds. Christ, the God-man, is a comfort to humanity. But, because of his very humanity, Christ is also a scandal that we stumble over. At times he is hard to take for real, for the burden of humanity is heavy. This was so when he was on earth, and it became so when he commissioned other men to spread his Good News in his name. People have left his Church, as they left him, because they both, at times, seemed all too human, too little divine. But more idealistic panaceas — democracy, nationalism, science, and socialism — have been weighed and found wanting. In the face of its options, if civilization is to endure, its response, like Peter's, will have to be: "To whom else can we go? You alone have the words of eternal life."

Discussion Questions

1. What is the difference between a club and the Church?
2. What does one mean when he refers to Christ's fragile fellowship as a "priestly people"?
3. Why make the Mass a celebration in English, serenaded by guitars?
4. How does Christ's Good News reinforce self-respect?
5. How can the Church better communicate the Good News in the modern world?

Index

181

Bibliography

General reference works:
New Catholic Encyclopedia, N. Y. 1967
Cross, F. L., ed., *The Oxford Dictionary of the Christian Church*, London, 1958
Danielou, J., ed., *The Christian Centuries: A New History of the Catholic Church*, N. Y., 1964
Daniel-Rops, Henri, *History of the Church of Christ*, New York, 1957-1967
Jedin, Hubert, *Handbook of Church History*, N. Y., 1965

Specialized subjects:
Delort, Robert, *Life in the Middle Ages*, N. Y., 1973
Grant, Robert M., *Augustus to Constantine: The Thrust of the Christian Movement into the Roman World*, N. Y., 1970
Heer, Friedrich, *The Medieval World*, N. Y., 1963
Obolensky, Dimitri, *The Byzantine Commonwealth: Eastern Europe, 500-1453*, N. Y., 1971
O'Connell, Marvin R., *The Counter Reformation, 1559-1610*, N. Y., 1974
Rhodes, Anthony, *The Vatican in the Age of the Dictators, 1922-1945*, N. Y., 1974
Tapie, Victor-L., *The Rise and Fall of the Habsburg Monarchy*, N. Y., 1971

THE ART OF CHOOSING
by Ronda Chervin, Ph.D.

An in-depth study of how our daily decisions affect our chance of becoming an ideal person. The author examines three types of persons to give us a better insight into the value of our own patterns of living. This book is recommended as a useful textbook for religion and philosophy classes and study groups. *96 pages, 8½ x 11, soft cover, $2.50.*

YOUR MARRIAGE
by John F. DeYonker, D.O.,
and Thomas E. Tobin, C.SS.R.

Details the purposes and responsibilities of a marriage, the influence each person's background has on the relationship, and the problems and privileges encountered. *144 pages, soft cover, $1.50.*

AN APPRECIATION OF EASTERN CHRISTIANITY
by Clement Englert, C.SS.R.

Explains the rites, laws, and customs of Eastern Christianity and how the liturgy and tradition differ from Roman Catholicism. The author explains problems that exist, and suggests possible solutions for eventual and total unity of Catholic and Orthodox Christians. *128 pages, soft cover, $1.95.*

CATHOLIC THOUGHT ON CONTRACEPTION
THROUGH THE CENTURIES
by Joseph A. Sommer, S.J., Ph.D.

The Church's teaching regarding contraception from early Scripture times to the present moment. Important for Catholics who must make personal and community decisions concerning contraception. *96 pages, soft cover, $1.25.*

CHURCH OF LOVE
by Ronda Chervin, Ph.D.
Shows how the sacraments, dogma, prayer, and other elements of the faith are evidence of God's love. The author uses a comparison of human and divine love to explain the Church. *144 pages, soft cover, $1.75.*

OUR DEBT TO THE FIRST CHRISTIANS
by Rev. Francis Timoney — 35c